Sara Chare, Andrew Swaffer
& Katrina O'Brien

Credits

Footprint credits
Editors: Alan Murphy, Nicola Gibbs
Layout and production: Angus Dawson
Maps: Kevin Feeney

Managing Director: Andy Riddle
Commercial Director: Patrick Dawson
Publisher: Alan Murphy
Publishing Managers: Felicity Laughton, Nicola Gibbs
Digital Editors: Jo Williams, Tom Mellors
Marketing and PR: Liz Harper
Sales: Diane McEntee
Advertising: Renu Sibal
Finance and Administration: Elizabeth Taylor

Photography credits
Front cover: Dejan Novkovski/Shutterstock
Back cover: Neale Cousland/Shutterstock

Printed in Great Britain by CPI Antony Rowe, Chippenham, Wiltshire

Every effort has been made to ensure that the facts in this guidebook are accurate. However, travellers should still obtain advice from consulates, airlines, etc about travel and visa requirements before travelling. The authors and publishers cannot accept responsibility for any loss, injury or inconvenience however caused.

Publishing information
Footprint *Focus Perth*
1st edition
© Footprint Handbooks Ltd
November 2011

ISBN: 978 1 908206 47 3
CIP DATA: A catalogue record for this book is available from the British Library

® Footprint Handbooks and the Footprint mark are a registered trademark of Footprint Handbooks Ltd

Published by Footprint
6 Riverside Court
Lower Bristol Road
Bath BA2 3DZ, UK
T +44 (0)1225 469141
F +44 (0)1225 469461
footprinttravelguides.com

Distributed in the USA by Globe Pequot Press, Guilford, Connecticut

The content of Footprint *Focus Perth* has been taken directly from Footprint's *West Coast Australia Handbook,* which was researched and written by Sara Chare, Andrew Swaffer and Katrina O'Brien.

Contents

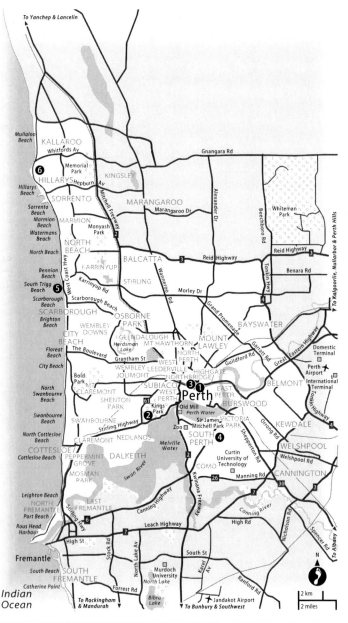

One of the most isolated cities in the world, Perth is a green, clean and spacious city on the banks of the wide, blue Swan River. The city is about three times the size of Greater London (with an eighth of the population), contained by coastline to the west and the low Perth Hills of the Darling Range to the east. It's a sparkling, modern place, reminiscent of American cities with its freeway, flyovers and dependence on the car.

Perth's best asset is an incredible climate. The sun simply never stops shining and each perfect sunny day is taken for granted. The endless expanse of blue sky and sea is a constant reflection in both the city's skyscrapers and residents' sunglasses. This makes for a city lived in the outdoors where the beaches, ocean, river and parks are the favourite haunts of the friendly, laid-back people of Perth.

Fremantle is Perth's port and effectively a suburb of the city. It is by no means eclipsed, however, and a visit to Perth is incomplete without time spent in this small historic outpost. It's also the principal jumping-off point for Rottnest Island, the penal settlement turned holiday playground. The Swan Valley is Perth's very own wine region and a pleasant place for lunch in a vine-covered courtyard on a sunny day.

Running parallel to the coast, about 30 km inland, the Perth Hills provide an extensive network of walking, mountain biking, and horse-riding tracks. It's from here that the Bibbulmun Track starts its winding 963-km route to Albany in the south. To the east lies the fertile Avon Valley where the Avon River flows through low, bare hills and pockets of woodland. Some of the state's oldest colonial settlements are found here, such as the charming town of York.

Planning your trip

When to go

Climate

The south, including Perth and the southwest, is sunny throughout spring, summer and autumn and these are the ideal seasons to visit. Perth gets an average of 7½ hours of sunshine a day. The southern winter lasts from June to August and this is when this region receives most of its rainfall and gets fairly cold (5-17°C). If you want to see whales though, it will have to be winter or spring when they migrate past the southwest coasts (June to November).

Weather forecasts: T1900 955366, www.bom.gov.au. Cyclone information: T1300 659210, www.bom.gov.au/weather/cyclone. Also useful is www.fesa.wa.gov.au.

Holidays and events

The main holidays start in mid-December and carry on through to the end of January. Schools also close for the two weeks after Easter, for two weeks in mid-July, and for another two weeks in early October. Backpackers don't need to be too concerned about visiting at these times as accommodation and tours aimed at that market are less affected.

WA's major festival, the Perth Festival, is held annually in January and February, and the start more or less coincides with state's biggest international sporting event, Tennis' Hopman Cup. ▸▸ *For public holidays and other important dates, see Festivals and events, page 15.*

Getting there

Air

There are international flights direct to Perth from many cities around the world as well as interstate ones from most other Australian state capitals, see Getting around, page 8. However, it is usually possible to book internal Australian flights when booking your international ticket, at lower prices than on arrival. Some do not even require a stated departure and arrival point. If you have any plans to fly within Australia check this out with your travel agent prior to booking.

Fares will depend on the season, with prices much higher during December-January unless booked well in advance. Mid-year tends to see the cheapest fares. Qantas and Virgin Blue are Australia's main international airlines and fly from a considerable number of international capitals and major cities. Most other major airlines have flights to Australia from their home countries or Europe.

From Europe The main route, and the cheapest, is via Asia, though fares will also be quoted via North America or Africa. The Asia route usually takes 20-24 hours including stops. There are as yet no non-stop routes (though Boeing's 787 could in theory do London to Perth in one hop), so it's worth checking out what stopovers are on offer: this might be your only chance to see Kuala Lumpur. Stopovers of a few nights do not usually increase the cost of the ticket appreciably. The cheapest return flights, off-season, will be around £700, with stand-by prices rising to at least £1400 around Christmas. Flights to Perth are usually marginally cheaper than to the other state capitals.

Don't miss ...

Airlines from Europe: **Air New Zealand**, www.airnz.co.uk; **British Airways**, www.british airways.com; **Cathay Pacific**, www.cathaypacific.com; **Emirates**, www.emirates.com; **Malaysia Airlines**, www.malaysiaairlines.com; **Qantas**, www.qantas.co.uk; **Singapore Airlines**, www.singaporeair.com; **Virgin Atlantic**, www.virgin-atlantic.com.

From North and South America There are direct **Qantas** flights from Los Angeles to Brisbane, Melbourne and Sydney, and from Vancouver and New York to Sydney. The cost of a standard return in the high season starts from around US$1500 from Vancouver, New York, and Los Angeles. There are also direct flights from Buenos Aires to Sydney.

Airlines from the Americas: **Air Canada**, www.aircanada.com; **Air New Zealand**, www.air newzealand.com; **Qantas**, www.qantas.com.au; **Singapore Airlines**, www.singapore air.com; **United**, www.united.com; **Virgin Atlantic**, www.virgin-atlantic.com.

From South Africa There are direct **Qantas** flights from Johannesburg to Perth. **South African Airways**, www.flysaa.com, also flies direct in around 11 hours.

Airport information
Perth Airport, www.perthairport.net.au, a little over 10 km east of the city centre, has two terminals: domestic and international. With no direct link between the two, transfers are via the perimeter highways (shuttle $8, transfer vouchers for passengers flying with Qantas or OneWorld available at Qantas ticketing counter, T9365 9777). The **domestic terminal**, Brearley Avenue, has a wide range of services including ATMs, **Travelex** foreign exchange, luggage lockers, cafés and all the major car hire firms. There are several transport options into Perth: a taxi costs around $30; the **Connect Airport Shuttle**, T1300 666 806, www.perthairportconnect.com.au, meets all flights ($15 one way, $25 return); the **Transperth** bus No 37 (bus stop opposite Qantas terminal, $3.70, 35 minutes) runs to the Esplanade Busport. Buses leave at least every 30 minutes (hourly after 1840) Monday-Friday 0600-2240; every 30-60 minutes on Saturday 0650-2240; and hourly on Sunday 0820-1820. The **international terminal**, Horrie Miller Drive, is slightly further out. Facilities are just as comprehensive and the **Thomas Cook** foreign exchange counters remain open before and after all flights. There is, however, no public bus route from this terminal, so it's either the shuttle ($18 one way, $30 return, details as above) or a taxi (about $35). There are also shuttles to Fremantle, T9457 7150, www.fremantleairport shuttle.com.au, and Scarborough, T0427 082652 (pre-booking required, $30-60).

Getting around

Both Perth and Fremantle have free city centre buses known as CATs (Central Area Transit), T136213, circulating the city on three different routes every seven to five minutes during the day and less regularly at night. **Transperth** ① *T136213, www.transperth.wa. gov.au, Mon-Thu 0500-2430, Fri-Sat 0500-0200, Sun 0500-2400*, operates the city's buses, trains and ferries and has several information centres where you can pick up timetables and ask for help. These are located at the Esplanade Busport, the main Railway Station and Wellington Street Bus Station. Urban bus routes tend to radiate out from the city centre, and travelling between peripheral areas, though usually possible, can be a tortuous affair. It is far simpler to take the train, services run regularly.

Wellington Street Bus Station is the main terminal for interstate coaches and some independent state services. **Greyhound** ① *East Perth Terminal, T1300 473946, www.greyhound.com.au*, runs the interstate services to Adelaide, Darwin and beyond. **TransWA** ① *T1300 662205 and T9326 2600, www.transwa.wa.gov.au*, operates most coach and train services within the state from the East Perth Terminal. The **Railway Station** on Wellington Street services the five suburban lines, while most metropolitan buses terminate at the **Esplanade Busport.** ›› *See Transport, page 55, for further details.*

City sightseeing ① *T9203 8882, www.citysightseeingperth.com.au, $27.50, children $10, concessions $22.50*, buses leave regularly throughout the day from major tourist sights in central Perth and operate a hop-on hop-off system. There is also the **City Explorer** ① *T9322 2006, www.perthtram.com.au, $30, children $12, concessions $25, sectional trips available for $8, children $4*, which offers a hop-on hop-off service by tram and open-top double-decker bus. The ticket is valid for two days and takes in Perth's major and historic attractions including Hay Street, Barrack Street Jetty, Kings Park, the Perth Mint and also stops at some of the major hotels.

As it's a fairly flat city Perth is ideal for cycling, see bike hire under Transport. Ferries sail from Barrack Street Jetty over to South Perth. ›› *See Transport, page 55.*

Vehicle hire   Car rental costs vary according to where you hire from (it's cheaper in Perth, though small local companies have good deals), what you hire and the mileage/insurance terms. You may be better off making arrangements in your own country for a fly-drive deal. Watch out for kilometre caps: some can be as low as 100 km per day. The minimum you'll pay is around $200 a week for a small car. Drivers need to be over 21. At peak times it can be impossible to hire at short notice, and some companies may dispose of a booked car within as little as half an hour of you not showing up for an agreed pick-up time. If you've booked a car but are going to be late ensure that you let them know. Some companies will offer one-way hire on certain models and under certain conditions.

Fuel   Fuel costs are approximately half that in Britain and nearly twice that in the USA, fluctuating between $1.30 a litre in and around Perth and at least 10% higher in the country. Anyone driving long distances in WA will soon find that fuel expenses exceed those of food and rival those of accommodation. Budget at least $20 for every estimated 100 km.

Hitchhiking

Hitchhiking, while not strictly illegal, is not advisable. There will always be the odd twisted soul around who will assault or abduct. This is not to say that hitching is more dangerous in WA than elsewhere else, but simply that bad things happen.

Orientation

The core of the city lines the banks of the Swan River from its mouth at Fremantle to the central business district (CBD), 19 km upstream, just north of an open basin known as Perth Water. Perth is contained by the coast to the west and the low 'Perth hills' of the Darling Ranges to the east, a corridor about 40 km wide. In the last 10 years the city has expanded rapidly along the sand dunes of the north coast to Joondalup and to the south almost as far as Rockingham. The northern suburbs, which are serviced by the freeway and the Joondalup train line, are a sea of new brick bungalows and modern shopping malls.

The oldest suburbs are those close to the river, particularly on the northern side such as Dalkeith and Peppermint Grove; these have always been the most wealthy and desirable places to live. The beach suburbs close to the city centre such as Cottesloe and City Beach are also affluent. Inner-city suburbs like Subiaco, Leederville and North Perth have become increasingly gentrified and sought after for their location and attractive old architecture.

The city centre is a small grid, just north of the river, of about 2 km by 1 km. The river is bordered by a strip of green lawn throughout the entire city area, and there is a walking trail alongside the river on both north and south banks. However, although the CBD faces the river, it is cut off from it by busy roads and freeways so the foreshore is not quite the asset it could be. South Perth is an attractive area with a wide grassy foreshore heavily used by joggers and picnickers. This is a fashionable suburb with many apartment blocks, making the most of views of the city skyline. Further south lies a large area of well-established middle-class suburbs around the Canning River and inland from Fremantle.

Tourist information

The **Perth Visitor Centre** ① *Forrest Pl, T9483 1111 and T1300 361 351, www.western australia.net, Mon-Thu 0830-1800, Fri 0830-1900, Sat 0930-1630, Sun 1200-1630*, is the main VIC for the state. You can pick up free maps and brochures for Perth and Fremantle, and booklets on each state region. It acts as a travel agent and sells national park passes. There is an **information kiosk** at the junction of Forrest Place and the Murray Street Mall; it's run by volunteers and not aimed specifically at tourists but it's a good place to ask for directions or advice. Free walking tours of the city leave from the kiosk Monday-Saturday at 1100 and Sunday at 1200. The **Traveller's Club** ① *92-94 Barrack St, T9226 0660, www.travellersclub.com.au, Mon-Sat 0900-2000, Sun 1000-2000*, is a very useful contact point for backpackers. It offers help and information, has travellers' noticeboards, cheap internet and acts as a tour booking centre. Aside from the VIC, information on national parks can be obtained from the **Department of Environment and Conservation (DEC)** ① *T9334 0333*. DEC produces a small brochure on each park and excellent publications on walking, fauna and flora. It is also possible to visit the **DEC information centre** ① *17 Dick Perry Av, Kensington, Mon-Fri 0800-1700*, to collect brochures, but this is out of the way.

Sleeping

There is a diverse and attractive range of accommodation options, from cheap national park campsites alive with wildlife to exclusive and luxurious retreats. Given the weather and the environment, travelling on a budget does not in any way detract from the enjoyment of a trip. On the contrary, this is a place where nights under canvas in national parks, or preparing your porridge on a campfire under the gaze of a possum is an absolute delight.

If we haven't provided the sleeping option to match your ideal, local VICs can supply full accommodation listings. Booking in advance is highly recommended, especially in peak seasons. Useful websites include: www.globalstore.com.au, www.jasons.com.au, www.travel.com.au and www.babs.com.au. Single rooms are relatively scarce outside of pubs, hostels and roadhouses. Air conditioning is common, but check when booking, and if they don't have it ask how they keep their rooms cool. There are plenty of rooms without air conditioning in Australia that are impossible to sleep in during hot weather.

Hotels, motels and resorts
At the top end of the scale are some impressive international-standard hotels and resorts, with luxurious surroundings and facilities, attentive service and often outstanding locations. Rooms will typically start in our $$$$ range. In the main cities are a few less expensive hotels in the $$$ range. Most 'hotels' outside the major towns are pubs with upstairs or external accommodation. If the room is upstairs it is likely to have access to shared bathroom facilities, while external rooms are usually standard en suite motel units. The quality of pub-hotel accommodation varies considerably, but is usually a budget option ($$). Linen is almost always supplied.

Motels in Australia are usually anonymous, but dependably clean and safe, and usually offer the cheapest en suite rooms. Most have dining facilities and free, secure parking. Some budget motels will fall into our $$ range, most will be $$$-$$. Linen is always supplied.

B&Bs and self-catering
Bed and Breakfast (B&B) is in some ways quite different from the British model. Not expensive, but rarely a budget option, most fall into our $$$-$$ ranges. They offer very comfortable accommodation in upmarket houses. Rooms are usually en suite or have access to a private bathroom. Bathrooms shared by more than two rooms are rare. Hosts are usually friendly and informative. Some B&Bs are actually a semi or fully self-contained cottage or cabin with breakfast provisions supplied. Larger ones may have full kitchens. As well as private houses, self-contained, self-catering options are provided by caravan parks and hostels, and some resorts and motels with apartment-style units. Check whether linen is supplied in self-catering accommodation.

National parks, farms and stations
Some national parks and rural cattle and sheep stations have old settlers or workers' homes that have been converted into accommodation, usually self-contained. They are often magical places to stay and include many old lighthouse keepers' cottages and shearers' quarters. Stations may also invite guests to see or even get involved in the day's activities. Transport to them can be difficult if you don't have your own. Linen is often not supplied in this sort of accommodation. See www.tacawa.com.au for information.

Hostels

Western Australia has a large network of good-value hostels (**$$-$**). They are popular centres for backpackers and provide a great opportunity for meeting fellow travellers. Most will have at least one double room and possibly singles, sometimes with linen. Almost all hostels have kitchen and common room facilities. A few, particularly in cities, will offer freebies including breakfast and pick-ups. Standards vary considerably, and it's well worth asking other travellers about the hostels at your next ports of call. Most are effectively independent and the best tend to be those that are owner-managed. International visitors can obtain a Hostelling International Card (HIC) from any YHA hostel or travel centre. For this you get a handbook to YHA hostels nationwide and around $3-4 off every night's YHA accommodation. The hostel associations **NOMADS** ① *T02-9280 4110, www.nomads world.com, no membership fee*, and **YHA** ① *www.yha.com.au*, seem to ensure the best consistency of quality. **YMCA** ① *T08-9473 8400, www.ymca.org.au*, and **YWCA** ① *T02-6230 5150, www.ywca.org.au*, hostels are usually a clean and quiet choice in the major cities.

Caravan and tourist parks

Almost every town will have at least one caravan park with unpowered and powered sites, varying from $10-25 for campers, caravans and campervans, a wash block and usually a camp kitchen or BBQs. Some will have permanently sited caravans (on-site vans) and cabins. On-site vans are usually the cheapest option (**$**) for families or small groups wanting to self-cater. Cabins are more expensive (**$$**). Some will have televisions, en suite bathrooms, separate bedrooms with linen and well-equipped kitchens. Power is rated at the domestic level (240/250v AC), which is convenient for budget travellers. Joining a park association will get you a discount in all parks that are association members. Associations include: **Big 4** ① *T03-9811 9300, www.big4.com.au*; **Family Parks of Australia** ① *T1300 855 707, www.familyparks.com.au*; and **Top Tourist Parks** ① *T08- 8363 1901, www.toptourist.contact.com.au*.

Campervans

A popular choice for many visitors is to hire or buy a vehicle that can be slept in, combining the costs of accommodation and transport (although you will still need to book into caravan parks for electricity and washing). Ranging from the popular VW Kombi to enormous vans with integral bathrooms, they can be hired from as little as $60 per day to as much as $1000. A van for two people at around $120 per day compares well with hiring a car and staying in hostels, and allows greater freedom. High-clearance 4WD campervans are also available, and increase travel possibilities yet further. Kombis can usually be bought from about $2500. A cheaper though less comfortable alternative is to buy a van or station wagon (estate car) that is big enough to sleep in.

Campervan companies Apollo ① *266 Great Eastern Highway, Belmont, T1800 777 779, www.apollocamper.com.au*; Backpacker ① *471 Great Eastern Highway, Redcliffe, T08-9479 5208, www.backpackercampervans.com*; Britz ① *471 Great Eastern Highway, Redcliffe, T08-9479 5208, www.britz.com*; Getabout ① *T02-9528 8015, www.getaboutoz.com*; Maui ① *471 Great Eastern Highway, Redcliffe, T08-9479 5208, www.maui-rentals.com*; Discover West ① *T08-6263 6475, www.discoverwest.com.au*; Wicked ① *T1800 246 869, www.wicked campers.com.au*. The latter are proving immensely popular with the backpacker set. However, they may not suit everyone (you'll see what we mean).

Eating and drinking

Food

The quintessential image of Australian cooking may be of throwing some meat on the barbie but Australia actually has a dynamic and vibrant cuisine all its own. Freed from the bland English 'meat and two veg' straitjacket in the 1980s by the skills and cuisines of Chinese, Thai, Vietnamese, Italian, Greek, Lebanese and other immigrants, Australia has developed a fusion cuisine that takes elements from their cultures and mixes them into something new and original. Asian ingredients are easily found in major cities because of the country's high Asian population and might include coriander, lemongrass, chilli, and Thai basil. Australia makes its own dairy products so cheese or cream may come from Tasmania's King Island or Margaret River. Of course there is also plenty of seafood, including some creatures that will be unfamiliar to most travellers like the delicious crustaceans: bugs, yabbies, and crayfish (lobster). Mussels, oysters and abalone are all also harvested locally. Fish is a treat too; try the firm white flesh of snapper, dhufish, coral trout and red emperor. WA's isolation and clean environment also ensures that all these ingredients taste as good as possible.

Freshness is the other striking quality of this cuisine, dubbed **Modern Australian**. This is achieved by using produce from the local area, and cooking it in a way that preserves the food's intrinsic flavour. The food shines for itself without being smothered in heavy or dominating sauces. Native animals are sometimes used, such as kangaroo, emu and crocodile, and native plants that Aboriginal people have been eating for thousands of years such as quandong, wattle seed or lemon myrtle leaf.

While you're licking your lips with anticipation: a word of warning. This gourmet experience is mostly restricted to Perth and the largest towns. There are pockets of foodie heaven in the southwest, but these are usually associated with wine regions and are the exception rather than the rule.

There are a few special foods that Australians produce and treasure and that can be found pretty much throughout WA. The **meat pie** is the favourite Australian fast food, about the size of your palm and filled with mince or steak and gravy. Quality can vary from soggy cardboard to something a French pastry chef wouldn't be ashamed of. If tempted, your best bet is a fresh one from a bakery rather than a mass-produced one (sealed in a little plastic bag) that sits in a shop's warming oven all day. **Fish and chips** are also popular and these are often good in Australia because the fish is fresh and only light vegetable oils are used for frying.

Vegemite spread is a dark and sticky yeast extract that looks a bit like axle grease. It's the Aussie equivalent of British Marmite, though fans of one usually detest the other. **Tim Tams** are a thick chocolate biscuit, very similar to the Brits' Penguin and reputedly the country's best-selling snack. What Brits call crisps, Aussies call chips ('hot chips' are fried chips), with **Twisties** a very Australian favourite.

Damper is bread made of flour, salt and water, best baked out bush in the ashes of a campfire. Nothing beats warm damper slathered with jam and butter. Another Aussie baking favourite is the **lamington**: a block of sponge that has been dipped in chocolate and rolled in coconut. The **pavlova** is a classic Australian dessert, created for the visit of Russian ballerina, Anna Pavlova. The 'pav' is like a cake-sized meringue, served topped with whipped cream and fresh fruit. It is rarely consumed without an argument about whether it was actually invented in Australia or New Zealand. One great icon associated with the outback campfire is **Billy Tea**. It is the fiendishly simple concept of putting a few eucalyptus leaves in with the brew to add that distinctive Aussie flavour. To mix the flavour of the tea leaf with the eucalypt the 'billy can' is held in the hand and swung a couple of times from the shoulders. This is quite a delicate art and can, for the uninitiated, result in considerable drama when the handle breaks.

Drink

Australian **wine** is now imported in huge quantities into Europe and the USA. The industry has a creditable history in such a young country, with several wineries boasting a tradition of a century or more, but it is only in the last 25 years that Australia has become one of the major players on the international scene. The price of wine is unexpectedly high given the relatively low cost of food and beer. Even those from Britain will find Australian wines hardly any cheaper at the very cellar door than back home in the supermarket. The joy of Australian wine, however, is in its variety and quality. There are no restrictions, as there are in parts of Europe, on what grape varieties are grown where, when they are harvested and how they are blended. The 'Mediterranean' climate of much of the south of the country is very favourable for grape-growing, and the soil is sufficient to produce a high-standard grape.

Wineries range in size from vast concerns to one-person operations producing a few hundred bottles a year. Cellars range from modern marble and glass temples to venerable, century-old former barns of stone and wood. Some will open for a Saturday afternoon, others every day. In some you'll be lucky to get half a dry cracker to go with a taste, others boast some of the best restaurants in the country. A few are in small town high streets, others are set in hectares of exquisitely designed and maintained gardens. The wonderful thing is that this tremendous mix of styles is found within most of the regions, making a day or two's tasting expedition a scenic and cultural as well as an Epicurean delight. WA has a handful of wine regions, one as far north as Geraldton and several along the south coast. The biggest are the **Swan Valley**, just outside Perth, and **Margaret River**, which is spread over much of the northern half of the Cape-to-Cape region. The latter is one of the most pleasant wine regions in the country. ▸▸ *See page for* *details of operators offering wine-tasting tours.*

The big two **beer** brands of WA are **Swan** and **Emu**, both are middle-of-the-road beers available in full and mid-strengths. The state also has a number of small independent brewers, one or two of which are becoming well known even outside the state. These include long-established **Matilda Bay**, producers of the popular **Redback**, and **Little Creatures** who are a little more creative than most of their peers and have a wonderful brewery/bar/restaurant/gallery in Fremantle. Pubs producing their own exceptionally good beers include the **Rose & Crown** in Guildford (see page 82). Beer is usually served in a 7 oz 'middy', though you can also ask for a 10 oz 'pot' or in some pubs a regular British-style pint. Beer tends to be around 4-5% alcohol, with the popular and surprisingly pleasant tasting 'mid' varieties about 3.5%, and 'light' beers about 2-2.5%. Drink-driving laws are strict, and the best bet is to not drink alcohol at all if you are driving. As well as being available on draught in pubs, beer is also available from bottleshops (or 'bottle-os') in cases (or 'slabs') of 24-36 cans ('tinnies' or 'tubes') or bottles ('stubbies') of 375 ml each. This is by *far* the cheapest way of buying beer (often under $1.50 per can or bottle).

Eating out

Restaurants are common even in smaller towns. It is a general, but by no means concrete rule of thumb that the smaller the town the lower the quality, though not usually the price. Chinese and Thai restaurants are very common, with most other cuisines appearing only in the larger towns and cities. In Perth and Fremantle you will find everything from Mexican to Mongolian, Jamaican to Japanese. Corporate hotels and motels almost all have attached restaurants as do traditional pubs which also serve counter meals. Some may have a more imaginative menu or better-quality fare than the local restaurants. Most restaurants are licensed for the consumption of alcohol. Some are BYO only, in which case you bring wine or beer and the restaurant provides glasses. Despite the corkage fee this still makes for a better deal than drinking alcohol in fully licensed premises. European-style cafés are only rarely found in the country, and as in many Western countries the distinction between cafés, bistros and restaurants is blurred.

If you can't do without your burgers or southern-fried chicken or fish and chips then fear not. Australians have taken to fast food as enthusiastically as anywhere else in the world. Alongside these are food courts, found in the shopping malls of cities and larger towns. These have several takeaway options, usually including various Asian cuisines, surrounding a central space equipped with tables and chairs. Also in the budget bracket are the delis and milk bars, also serving hot takeaways, together with sandwiches, cakes and snacks. These make up a fair proportion of the country's cafés, with a few seats inside and often out on the pavement.

If you cook for yourself you'll find just about everything in an Aussie supermarket that you would find in Europe or the USA, and at very reasonable prices. An excellent meal for two can easily be put together for under $25.

Entertainment

As in most Western nations, much of the country's entertainment is provided by its **pubs** and **bars**. Not only are they a social meeting point but many put on regular live music, DJs, karaoke and quiz nights. The typical Aussie pub is a solid brick and wood affair with wide first-floor verandas extending across the front, and sometimes down the sides as well. These usually have separate public and lounge bars, a bottleshop (off-licence) off to the side, and increasingly a separate 'bar' full of pokies (slot machines or one-armed bandits). The public bar often doubles as a TAB betting shop. Pubs and bars vary as much in style as anywhere in the western world. Some pubs are rough as guts and a stranger venturing in is guaranteed a hard stare. Others go out of their way to make a visitor feel welcome. Some haven't seen a paintbrush since the day they were built, others have been beautifully renovated in styles ranging from modern to authentic outback, saloon to the gimmicky Irish. In some medium-sized towns they also operate a club or discotheque. True **nightclubs** will only be found in the cities and larger towns, and then usually only open a few nights of the week. They do generally charge an entrance fee, usually around $10-20, though entry will commonly be free on some mid-week nights or before a certain time.

The **cinema** is popular in Australia and some will have outdoor screens with either deckchair seating or drive-in slots. Expect to pay $15-20 for an adult ticket, but look out for early week or pre-1800 specials. Every big city in the country has its major **casino**. Most are open 24 hours a day and, as well as offering gaming tables and rank upon rank of pokies, also have live music venues and good-value food halls and restaurants.

Other indoor pursuits found in most large towns and cities include ten-pin bowling, bingo, karting, snooker and pool halls, and large recreational centres offering everything from swimming to squash, basketball to badminton.

Festivals and events

Most major events and festivals are held in and around Perth, where nearly three quarters of Western Australians live. The year kicks off with the **Hopman Cup**, www.hopmancup. com.au, an international tennis championship that attracts some big tennis names with its unusual format: teams of one male and one female player representing eight nations competing in a 'round robin' format. It is held at Perth's Burswood Dome over New Year. The arts year starts in January-February with the biggest and the best: **Perth International Arts Festival**, www.perthfestival.com.au. This includes local and international theatre, opera, dance, visual arts, film and music. Down in Margaret River the main event of the summer is the **Leeuwin Estate Concert**, www.leeuwinestate.com.au, held over a weekend in February, when sees musical performances given in the lovely grounds of this premium winery. Attracting quite a different crowd, the **Margaret River Salomon Masters** international surfing competition is held at Prevelly over a week in mid-April. Waves are also the focus of the **Avon Descent** in early August, a 133-km whitewater competition on the Avon River from Northam to Perth. Up north, Broome celebrates the Festival of the Pearl, **Shinju Matsuri**, for a week in late August or early September. Events include parades, dragon boat racing and the Shinju Ball. In spring, wildflowers are out all over the state but if you are short of time you can see many varieties at the **Kings Park Festival**, held in September. In the southwest, the **Bridgetown Blues Festival** is held in late November. See www.westernaustralia.com, for exact dates of forthcoming events.

Public holidays

New Year's Day 1 Jan; **Australia Day** 26 Jan 2011, 26 Jan 2012, 28 Jan 2013; **Labour Day**, 7 Mar 2011, 5 Mar 2012, 4 Mar 2013; **Good Friday**, 22 Apr 2011, 6 Apr 2012; **Easter Monday**, 25 Apr 2011, 9 Apr 2012; **Anzac Day**, 25 and 26 Apr 2011, 25 Apr 2012; **Foundation Day**, 6 Jun 2011, 4 Jun 2012; **Queen's Birthday**, 3 Oct 2011, 1 Oct 2012; **Christmas Day** 25 Dec; **Boxing Day** 26 Dec.

Essentials A-Z

Accident and emergency

Dial 000 for the emergency services.
The 3 main professional emergency services are supported by several others, including the **State Emergency Service (SES)**, **Country Fire Service (CFS)**, **Surf Life Saving Australia (SLSA)**, **Sea-search and Rescue**, and **St John's Ambulance**. The **SES** is prominent in co-ordinating search-and-rescue operations. The **CFS** provides invaluable support in fighting and controlling bush fires. These services, though professionally trained, are mostly provided by volunteers. Seasonal fire bans are managed by local shires. Contact the shire directly or the nearest VIC for advice.

Customs and duty free

The limits for duty-free goods brought into the country include: 2.25 litres of any alcoholic drink (beer, wine or spirits), and 250 cigarettes, or 250 g of cigars or tobacco. There are various import restrictions, mainly there to help protect Australia's already heavily hit ecology. These primarily involve live plants and animals, plant and animal materials (including all items made from wood) and foodstuffs. If in doubt, confine wooden and plant goods to well-worked items and bring processed food only (even this may be confiscated, though Marmite is accepted with a knowing smile). Muddy walking boots may also attract attention. Declare any such items for inspection on arrival if you are unsure. See www.customs.gov.au for more details.

Electricity

The current in Australia is 240/250v AC. Plugs have 2- or 3-blade pins and adaptors are widely available.

Embassies and commissions

For a list of Australian embassies and high commissions worldwide and foreign embassies and consulates in Australia, see http://.embassy.goabroad.com.

Health

UK also enjoy subsidized out-of-hospital treatment (ie visiting a doctor). All visitors to Australia are, however, strongly advised to get medical insurance.

See your doctor or travel clinic at least 6 weeks before your departure for advice on health risks. Make sure you have travel insurance, get a dental check (especially if you are going to be away for more than a month), know your own blood group and if you suffer a long-term condition such as diabetes or epilepsy, make sure someone knows or that you have a **Medic Alert** bracelet/necklace.

Health risks

Dengue fever can be contracted throughout Australia. In travellers this can cause a severe flu-like illness, which includes symptoms of fever, lethargy, enlarged lymph glands and muscle pains. It starts suddenly, lasts for 2-3 days, seems to get better for 2-3 days and then kicks in again for another 2-3 days. It is usually all over in an unpleasant week. The local children are prone to the much nastier haemorrhagic form of the disease, which causes them to bleed from internal organs, mucous membranes and often leading to death. The traveller's version of the disease is self-limiting and forces rest and recuperation on the sufferer. The mosquitoes that carry the dengue virus bite during the day unlike the malaria mosquitoes. Repellent application and covered limbs are a 24-hr issue.

Hepatitis means inflammation of the liver. Viral causes of the disease can be acquired anywhere in Australia. The most obvious symptom is a yellowing of your skin or the whites of your eyes. However, prior to this all that you may notice is itching and tiredness. Early on, depending on the type of hepatitis, a vaccine or immunoglobulin may reduce the duration of the illness. Hepatitis A is transmitted through food or water contaminated by faeces; a pre-travel vaccine is the best prevention. Hepatitis B (for which there is also a vaccine) is spread through blood and unprotected sexual intercourse, both of these can be avoided. Unfortunately there is no vaccine for Hepatitis C or the increasing alphabetical list of other Hepatitis viruses.

Snakes and other poisonous things are always a risk in Australia. A bite itself does not mean that anything has been injected in to you. However, a commonsense approach is to clean the area of the bite (never have it sutured early on) and get someone to take you to a medical facility as soon as possible. Keep calm and still: the more energy you expend the faster poisons spread. Do not try to catch the snake or spider but it is helpful if you can described what it looks like. For some snake bites a knowledgeable first aider can provide appropriate bandaging. Specialist anti-venoms will be administered by an experienced doctor.

In terms of **sexual health**, unprotected sex can obviously spread HIV, Hepatitis B and C, gonorrhea (green discharge), chlamydia (nothing to see but may cause painful urination and later female infertility), painful recurrent herpes, syphilis and warts, just to name a few. You can cut down the risk by using condoms, a femidom or avoiding sex altogether. Commercial sex workers in Australia have high levels of HIV. If you do have sex, consider getting a sexual health check on your return home.

Take care with **sun protection**. Sunburn is painful and followed by flaking of skin. Aloe vera gel is a good pain reliever. Long-term sun damage leads to a loss of elasticity of skin and the development of pre-cancerous lesions. Many years later a mild or a very malignant form of cancer may develop. The milder basal cell carcinoma, if detected early, can be treated by cutting it out or freezing it. The much nastier malignant melanoma may have already spread to bone and brain at the time that it is first noticed. SPF stands for Sun Protection Factor. The higher the SPF the greater the protection. However, do not use higher factors just to stay out in the sun longer. 'Flash frying' (desperate bursts of excessive exposure) is known to increase the risks of skin cancer. Follow the Australians' with their Slip, Slap, Slop campaign.

Australia has the 4th lowest level in the world for **tuberculosis** and is well protected by health screens before people can settle there. Symptoms include a cough, tiredness, fever and lethargy. Have a BCG vaccination before you go and see a doctor early if you cough blood or have a persistent cough, fever or unexplained weight loss.

Underwater health if you go diving make sure that you are fit do so. **British Scuba Association** (BSAC) in the UK (T01513-506200, www.bsac.com) can put you in touch with doctors who do medical examinations. Check that any dive company you use know what they are doing, have appropriate certification from BSAC or PADI, (www.padi.com), and that the equipment is well maintained. Protect your feet from cuts, beach dog parasites (larva migrans) and sea urchins. The latter are almost impossible to remove but can be dissolved with lime or vinegar. Keep an eye out for secondary infection. See the boxes on pages and for further details about keeping safe on land and in the sea.

Medical services

Medical services are listed in the Directory section of the relevant areas in this guide.

There are numerous hospitals, pharmacies and medical centres across the west coast.

Useful websites
www.btha.org British Travel Health Association (UK). The official website of an organization of travel health professionals. **www.cdc.gov** US Government site that gives excellent advice on travel health and details of disease outbreaks. **www.fitfortravel.scot.nhs.uk** A-Z of vaccine/health advice for each country. **www.who.int** The WHO Blue Book lists the diseases of the world.

Insurance
It's a very good idea to take out some form of travel insurance, wherever you're travelling from. This should cover you for theft or loss of possessions and money, the cost of medical and dental treatment, cancellation of flights, delays in travel arrangements, accidents, missed departures, lost baggage, lost passport and personal liability and legal expenses. Also check on inclusion of 'dangerous activities' such as climbing, diving, skiing, horse riding, even trekking, if you plan on doing any.

You should always read the small print carefully. Not all policies cover ambulance, helicopter rescue or emergency flights home. Find out if your policy pays medical expenses direct to the hospital or doctor, or if you have to pay and then claim the money back later. If the latter applies, make sure you keep all records. There are a variety of policies to choose from, so it's best to shop around. Your travel agent can advise on the best deals.

If you are unfortunate enough to have something stolen, make sure you get a copy of the police report, as you will need this to substantiate your claim.

Companies include: **Access America**, T1800 284 8300, www.accessamerica.com. (In USA). **Age Concern,** T0800 009966,

www.ageconcern.org.uk. (For older travellers in UK). **Columbus**, T0870 033 9988, www.columbusdirect.com. (In UK). **Direct Travel Insurance**, T0845 605 2700, www.direct-travel.co.uk. (In UK). **Flexicover Group**, T0845 223 4520, www.flexicover.co.uk. (In UK). **STA**, T800 7814040, www.statravel.com. (In USA). **Travel Insurance Services**, T800 9371387, www.travelinsure.com. (In USA).

Internet
Internet access, and thus email, is widely available in hostels, hotels and cafés. Expect to pay $2-5 for 30 mins.

Money
→ *Exchange rates (Sep 2011): US$1 = Aus$0.96, £1 = Aus$1.53, € 1 = Aus$1.32.*
All dollars quoted in this guide are Australian unless specified otherwise.
The Australian dollar ($) is divided into 100 cents (c). Coins come in denominations of 5c, 10c, 20c, 50c, $1 and $2. Banknotes come in denominations of $5, $10, $20, $50 and $100.

Banks
The 4 major banks, **Westpac, Commonwealth, NAB** and **ANZ**, are usually the best places to change money (and traveller's cheques), though bureaux de change tend to have slightly longer opening hours and often open at weekends. Typical bank opening hours are Mon-Fri 0930-1630.

Cost of living/travelling
Accommodation, particularly outside Perth, is good value, though prices can rise uncomfortably in peak seasons. Eating out can be indecently cheap. Around $175 is enough to cover dinner for 2 at the very best restaurants in Perth and the bill at many still excellent establishments can be half that. Transport varies considerably in price and can be a major factor in your travelling budget.

Beer is about $5-8 a throw in pubs and bars, as is a neat spirit or glass of wine. Wine will generally be around 1½ times to double the price in restaurants as it would be from a bottleshop. The general cost of living in Australia is reckoned to be equivalent to the USA and slightly cheaper than the UK.

The minimum budget required, if staying in hostels or campsites, cooking for yourself, not drinking much and travelling relatively slowly is about $90 per person per day, but this isn't going to be a lot of fun. Going on the odd tour, travelling faster and eating out occasionally will raise this to a more realistic $110-140. Those staying in modest B&Bs, hotels and motels as couples, eating out most nights and taking a few tours will need to reckon on about $200-300 per person per day. Non-hostelling single travellers should budget on spending around 60-70% of what a couple would spend.

Debit and credit cards

You can withdraw cash from **ATMs** (cashpoints) with a debit or credit card issued by most international banks. Most hotels, shops, tourist operators and restaurants in Australia accept the major credit cards, though some places may charge for using them. When booking always check if an operator accepts them.

If you need money urgently, the quickest way to have it sent is to have it wired to the nearest bank via **Western Union**, T1800 173833, www.westernunion.com. Charges apply but on a sliding scale. Complete online services are available with **Travelex**, www.travelex.com.au. Money can also be wired by **Amex** or **Thomas Cook**, though this may take a day or 2, or transferred direct from bank to bank, but this can take several days. Within Australia money orders can be used to send money, www.auspost.com.au.

Discounts

Many forms of transport and most tourist sites and tours will give discounts to all or some of the following: students, backpackers, the unemployed, the aged (all grouped as 'concessions' in this guide) and children. Proof will be required, a passport is usually sufficient for children or the aged.

Traveller's cheques

The safest way to carry money is in traveller's cheques, though travellers' dependence on them is fast becoming superseded by the prevalence of ATMs. **American Express**, **Thomas Cook** and **Visa** are the cheques most commonly accepted. Remember to keep a record of the cheque numbers and the cheques you've cashed separate from the cheques themselves. Traveller's cheques are accepted for exchange in banks, large hotels, post offices and large gift shops. Some insist that at least a portion of the amount is in exchange for goods or services. Commission when cashing traveller's cheques is usually 1% or a flat rate. Hotel rates are often poor.

Opening hours

Office and shop hours are typically Mon-Fri 0830-1700. Many convenience stores and supermarkets are open daily. Late-night shopping is generally Thu or Fri. See also under Banks and Post offices.

Post

Most post offices are open Mon-Fri 0900-1700, and Sat 0900-1230. Sending a postcard, greeting card or 'small' letter (less than 130 x 240 mm, 5 mm thick and 250 g) anywhere in Australia is $0.60 and should arrive within 3 days. Airmail for postcards and greetings cards is $1.45 anywhere in the world, small letters (under 50 g) from $1.50 (USA/UK: $2.20). Parcels can be sent by sea or air. Most of the principal or main offices in major towns and cities offer **Post Restante** for those peripatetic and quixotic travellers with no fixed address who still receive physical post.

Safety

In Perth and the other major cities, as in almost any city in the world, there is always the possibility of muggings, alcohol-induced harassment or worse. The usual simple precautions apply, like keeping a careful eye and hand on belongings, not venturing out alone at night and avoiding dark, lonely areas. Footprint is a partner in the Foreign and Commonwealth Office's 'Know before you go' campaign, www.fco.gov.uk/travel.

Student travellers

If you're a student make sure you have identification as it will be a ticket to much in the way of discounted accommodation, tours and more. There are various official youth/ student ID cards available, including the widely recognized **International Student ID Card (ISIC)** and **International Youth Travel Card (IYTC)**, both available from www.isic.org. Also the **Euro 26 Card**, www.euro26.org, and **Go-25 Card**. Each conveys benefits from simply getting discounts, to emergency medical coverage and 24-hr hotlines. The cards are issued by student travel agencies and hostelling organizations. Backpackers will find a YHA or VIP membership card just as useful.

Tax

There are currently a number of **departure taxes** levied by individual airports (such as noise tax) and the government. All departure taxes are included in the cost of a ticket, but may not be included in a quote when you first enquire about the cost of a ticket. Almost all goods in Australia are subject to a **Goods and Services Tax (GST)** of 10%. Visitors from outside Australia will find certain shops can deduct the GST if you have a departure ticket.

Telephone

→ *Country code: +61. Western Australia code: 08, followed by an 8-digit number.*

Most public payphones are operated by **Telstra**, www.telstra.com.au. Some take phonecards, available from newsagents and post offices, and credit cards. A payphone call within Australia requires $0.50. If you are calling locally (within approximately 50 km) this lasts indefinitely. **STD** calls outside this area will use up your 50c in less than a minute and cost about 1c a second thereafter.

There are no area phone codes, but you will need to use a **state code** for numbers in: ACT/NSW (**02**); VIC/TAS (**03**); QLD (**07**).

To call **Western Australia** from overseas, dial the international prefix followed by 618, then the 8-digit number. To call WA from ACT/NSW/VIC/TAS/QLD, dial 08 followed by the 8-digit number. You can access the national database of telephone numbers and their accompanying addresses at www.whitepages.com.au. The *Yellow Pages* is at www.yellowpages.com.au.

To call **overseas from Australia** dial 0011 followed by the country code. Country codes include: **Republic of Ireland** 353; **New Zealand** 64; **South Africa** 27; the **USA** and **Canada** 1; the **UK** 44. By far the cheapest way of calling overseas is to use an international pre-paid phonecard (cannot be used from a mobile phone, or some of the blue and orange public phones), unless you can find somewhere offering Skype.

Worth considering if you are in Australia for any length of time is a **pre-paid mobile phone. Telstra** and **Vodaphone** give the best coverage and widely available for less than $100. Calls are more expensive, of course.

Time

Western Standard Time: GMT+8 hrs. 1½ hrs behind SA and the NT, 2 hrs behind the eastern states. Daylight Saving from Apr-Oct is GMT + 9 hrs.

Tourist information

Tourist offices, or **Visitor Information Centres (VICs)**, can be found in all but the smallest Western Australian towns. Their locations, phone numbers, website or email addresses, and opening hours are listed in the relevant sections of this guide. In most larger towns they have to have met certain criteria to be officially *accredited*. This usually means that they have some paid staff and will almost certainly mean they are open daily 0900-1700 (except, usually, Christmas Day). Smaller offices may close at weekends, but given that many are run entirely by volunteers something to bear in mind when someone struggles to find an obscure piece of information the level of commitment to the visitor is impressive. All offices will provide information on accommodation, and local sights, attractions, and tours. Many will also have information on eating, local history and the environment, and sell souvenirs, guides and maps. Most will provide a free town map.

Weights and measures

All metric.

Visas and immigration

Visas are subject to change, so check first with your local Australian Embassy or High Commission. All travellers to Australia, except New Zealand citizens, must have a valid visa to enter Australia. These must be arranged prior to travel (allow 2 months) and cannot be organized at Australian airports.

Tourist visas are free and are available from your local Australian Embassy or High Commission, or in some countries, in electronic format (an Electronic Travel Authority or ETA) from their websites, and from selected travel agents and airlines. Passport holders eligible to apply for an ETA include those from Austria, Belgium, Canada, Denmark, Finland, France, Germany, Greece, Hong Kong, the Irish Republic, Italy, Japan, Netherlands, Norway, Spain, Sweden, Switzerland, the UK and the USA. Tourist visas allow visits of up to 3 months within the year after the visa is issued. 6-month, multiple-entry tourist visas are also available to visitors from certain countries. Tourist visas do not allow the holder to work in Australia. See also www.immi.gov.au.

The **working holiday visa**, which must also be arranged prior to departure, is available to people aged 18 to 30 from certain countries that have reciprocal arrangements with Australia, including Canada, Denmark, France, Germany, Irish Republic, Italy, Japan, Korea, Netherlands, Norway, Sweden, Taiwan and the UK. The working holiday visa allows multiple entries for 1 year from first arrival. It is granted on the condition that the holder works for no more than 3 months for a single employer. Your local Australian Embassy or High Commission issues the visa, for which there is a charge. Application forms can be downloaded from www.immi.gov.au.

Contents

Perth

Sights

Perth is primarily an outdoor city. A place to soak up the perfect sunny climate by going to the beach, sailing on the Swan River or walking in Kings Park. The city has few grand public institutions and much of its early colonial architecture has been demolished to create a glossy modern city. The most impressive cultural sights are gathered together in the plaza called the Cultural Centre, just north of the railway line in Northbridge. The Art Gallery and the Western Australian Museum are both excellent and give a fine insight into the history and culture of the state. Kings Park, just west of the city centre, is the largest green space close to any state capital and is the city's most popular attraction. The park is regularly used by the locals for its views, peaceful walks and picnic spots, café and outdoor cinema. Swan Bells tower also has good city views, and can easily be combined with a visit to Perth Zoo, which is an unexpected oasis of bush and jungle set back from the river shore of South Perth.

Central Perth and Northbridge » *For listings, see pages 35-58.*

The city centre is laid out in a grid just north of the river. Four main streets run east–west within this grid. St George's Terrace is the commercial district, full of skyscrapers and offices. Hay and Murray streets are the shopping and eating streets, while Wellington borders the railway line and is slightly seedier. Just north of the railway line is Northbridge. This is reached by a walkway from Forrest Place, over Wellington Street and the Perth train station to the Cultural Centre. Northbridge lies just to the west of the plaza, bordered by William Street. This whole area is undergoing regeneration, with a lot of building work and land-scaping taking place around the Cultural Centre. The main shopping district is contained within the Hay and Murray Street Malls and the arcades running between the malls.

Art Gallery of Western Australia

ⓘ *Perth Cultural Centre, T9492 6600 and T9492 6644 (for bookings), www.artgallery.wa. gov.au, Wed-Mon 1000-1700, free; guided tours run most days, Blue CAT route, stop 7, walkway to Perth train station, car parking within the Perth Cultural Centre precinct.*
The gallery forms the southern point of the **Cultural Centre** triangle of public institutions. The main gallery was built in 1979 to house the **State Art Collection** and the clean lines of its featureless exterior walls conceal cool white hexagonal spaces inside. The ground floor is used for temporary exhibitions and this is where the state's most prestigious visiting

exhibitions are shown. The central spiral staircase leads to the Aboriginal Art and Contemporary Art collections on the first floor. The gallery's collection of **Aboriginal Art** is one of the most extensive and impressive in Australia, encompassing bark paintings from Arnhem Land, dot paintings by Central Desert artists and works by WA artists such as Jimmy Pike and Sally Morgan. This collection is enhanced by detailed explanations of each painting and biography of the artist. The **Contemporary Art** collection also includes the best of craft and design in ceramics, glass, furniture and metalwork. More traditional work can be seen in the **Centenary Galleries** in the elegant former Police Court building (1905). The emphasis is on Western Australian art from colonial times to the present but also includes painters such as John Glover, Eugene Von Guérard, and Frederick McCubbin's iconic *Down on His Luck*, 1887. The gallery has an excellent shop stocking fine craft work and a huge range of art books. The spacious, relaxed café opposite does good casual Mediterranean-style food (Monday-Friday 0800-1700, Saturday-Sunday 0900-1700).

Perth Institute of Contemporary Arts (PICA)

ⓘ *Perth Cultural Centre, T9228 6300, www.pica.org.au, Tue-Sun 1100-1800, free entry, Blue CAT route, stop 7.*

Just down the steps from the Art Gallery is PICA, which showcases Australian and international visual, performance and cross-disciplinary art. The exhibitions change regularly and there are performances of contemporary dance and theatre to be enjoyed. PICA prides itself on nurturing new talent and challenging its visitors. The artwork may not be to everyone's tastes, but visit the website to see what's on or just head down and take a look.

State Library of Western Australia

ⓘ *Perth Cultural Centre, T9427 3111, www.slwa.wa.gov.au, Mon-Thu 0900- 2000, Fri 0900-1730, Sat-Sun 1000-1730, book to use internet (1 hr) or queue for an express computer (20 mins usage), Blue CAT route, stop 7.*

Opposite the Art Gallery is the complementary modern architecture of the state reference library. The **JS Battye Library**, on the third level, is a comprehensive collection of WA history titles and archives. Recent national and international newspapers and magazines can be read on the ground floor, where there is also free internet access. The **State Film and Video Archive** is on the second level and visitors can choose a film from the catalogue and use the viewing facilities on request. Other facilities include a café, lockers and a discard bookshop selling ex-library books. The library shop stocks the city's best range of books on WA.

Western Australian Museum

ⓘ *Perth Cultural Centre, T9212 3700, www.museum.wa.gov.au, 0930-1700, free, Blue CAT route, stop 7.*

The natural science collection of the Western Australian Museum came together during the gold boom of the 1890s when the new settlers had the money to think up fine public facilities. The site held the combined functions of the state library, museum and art gallery until 1955 and sprawls over a large area containing many different architectural styles. The main entrance on James Street joins the Jubilee Building and Hackett Hall. The Jubilee Building was built in 1899 in Victorian Byzantine style, from Rottnest and Cottesloe sandstone. It houses the **Mammal Gallery**, which still displays specimens in

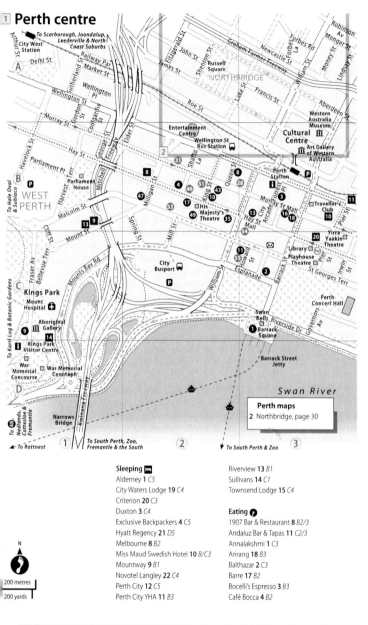

Perth centre

Sleeping 🛏
Alderney **1** C5
City Waters Lodge **19** C4
Criterion **20** C3
Duxton **3** C4
Exclusive Backpackers **4** C5
Hyatt Regency **21** D5
Melbourne **8** B2
Miss Maud Swedish Hotel **10** B/C3
Mountway **9** B1
Novotel Langley **22** C4
Perth City **12** C5
Perth City YHA **11** B3

Riverview **13** B1
Sullivans **14** C1
Townsend Lodge **15** C4

Eating 🍴
1907 Bar & Restaurant **8** B2/3
Andaluz Bar & Tapas **11** C2/3
Annalakshmi **1** C3
Arirang **18** B3
Balthazar **2** C3
Barre **17** B2
Bocelli's Espresso **3** B3
Café Bocca **4** B2

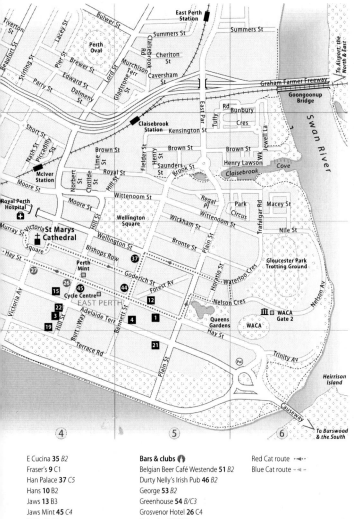

E Cucina **35** *B2*
Fraser's **9** *C1*
Han Palace **37** *C5*
Hans **10** *B2*
Jaws **13** *B3*
Jaws Mint **45** *C4*
Mai's **44** *C5*
Matsuri **47** *B2*
Merchant Tea &
  Coffee Company **16** *B3*
Old Swan Brewery **48** *D1*
Tiger Tiger Coffee Bar **43** *B2*
Velvet Espresso **49** *B2*

Bars & clubs 🍸
Belgian Beer Café Westende **51** *B2*
Durty Nelly's Irish Pub **46** *B2*
George **53** *B2*
Greenhouse **54** *B/C3*
Grosvenor Hotel **26** *C4*
Helvetica **55** *C2/3*
Hula Bula **27** *C4*
Moon & Sixpence **28** *B2/3*
Tiger Lil's **31** *B2*

Red Cat route ⤍⤍⤍
Blue Cat route ⤏ ⤏

their cedar and glass cases from 1903 and bird, butterfly and marine galleries. Visitors will also find the **Diamonds to Dinosaurs Gallery** here, where they will be taken on a journey through time from the origins of the universe to the evolution of life on Earth. Some of the fossils on display are incredible. The beautiful Hackett Hall was built to house the library in 1903 and still retains the original fittings, now a backdrop to the museum's best exhibition, *WA Land and People*. This is a contemporary look at Western Australia from its ancient geological beginnings to Aboriginal life, European invasion and the ways in which the land has both shaped and been shaped by its residents. The fascinating **Aboriginal Gallery** is in the Beaufort Street Gallery, the former art gallery. This is called Katta Djinoong, meaning 'see us and understand us' and goes a long way towards its aim. The exhibition examines the past and present of WA's different indigenous groups, and contemporary issues such as the 'stolen generation'. Displays on the European history of WA are shown in the Old Gaol, which was built by convicts as a gaol and courthouse and used until 1899 when the prisoners were transferred to Fremantle gaol. Beyond the gaol is the Megamouth shark display. The **museum shop** ① *Mon-Fri 1000-1645, Sat-Sun 1100-1645*, has a good range of books, as well as gifts and museum souvenirs. There is also a **café** ① *Mon-Fri 0930-1600, Sat-Sun 1100-1600*, for light snacks and drinks.

Perth Mint

① *310 Hay St, T9421 7223, www.perthmint.com.au/visit, Mon-Fri 0900-1700, Sat-Sun 0900-1300, tours every hour Mon-Fri0930-1530, Sat-Sun 0930-1130, gold pours on the hour, entry and tours $15, children $5, concessions $13, Red CAT route, stop 11.*

During the 19th century London's Royal Mint established three branches in Australia. The last to be opened, just two years before Federation, was in Perth as a direct result of the gold-rushes that were then gripping the colony and stripping it of ready currency. Built of Rottnest limestone the buildings have endured and the work of the mint has continued to the present day. Although it no longer produces day-to-day currency, it is still the major refiner of WA gold and buys and sells it at market prices. They also mint a wide range of commemorative medals and coins. Several display rooms are open to the public. Some have windows through to the production area, others contain some of WA's most historic and largest nuggets, and one contains a solid 400 oz gold bar. It's half as big as a house brick but about 10 times as hard to pick up, and you're allowed to have a try. There are regular guided tours and some culminate in a live 'gold pour', quite a spectacular sight.

Swan Bells

① *Barrack Sq, T6210 0444, www.ringmybells.com.au, daily from 1000 (closing times vary seasonally), $11, children and concessions $8, the bells are rung Sat-Tue and Thu 1200-1300 and visitors can have a go Wed and Fri 1130-1230, Blue CAT route, stop 19.*

It is little known in England that the church bells of St Martin-in-the-Fields, the ones that ring in the new year at Trafalgar Square, are almost brand new and made from Western Australian metals. The original bells, cast in the 1700s from bell metal that was possibly first poured a thousand years ago and used to celebrate Captain Cook's home-coming, were found to be stressing the church tower, and it was decided to gift them to WA to commemorate Australia's bicentenary in 1988. Exerting a force of over 40 tonnes, the bells needed a substantial bell-tower to house them. Perth not only provided just that, but made the tower the centrepiece of Old Perth Port, a striking, sweeping construction soaring 80 m with twin, copper-clad sails. The bell-chamber is easily accessed and walled with almost sound-proof doubled-glazed windows. These are now the only church bells in the world you can watch without being deafened.

Kings Park
ⓘ T9480 3659, www.bgpa.wa.gov.au, 0930-1600, free, No 33 bus from St Georges Terr to Fraser Av or Blue CAT bus to stop 21 and walk up Jacob's Ladder.

This huge playground for the city and central suburbs is just about everything you could want a park to be. A large area of natural bush, threaded through with unsigned bush walks, is bordered to the south and east by broad bands of carefully manicured lawns and gardens, these in turn encompassing the excellent **Botanic Gardens**. From many of these are tremendous views across to the city centre and Barrack Street jetty, particularly beautiful at sunset, and very popular with picnickers. The main visitor area is at the end of Fraser Avenue, opposite the **State War Memorial**, one of many memorials in the park as well as one of the best city-viewing spots. There's a **kiosk** ⓘ daily 0900-1700, some superb tea-rooms and restaurants, the visitor centre and public toilets. Here you can pick up a map of the park, self-guided walking maps, and details of the various events and activities.

There are free guided walks from the old Karri log near the centre every day at 1000 and 1400 (bookings not necessary), usually focusing on either the Botanic Gardens or the history of the park, but with variations in winter and spring looking at the local wildflowers and bushland. Walks usually take about 1½ hours, bushland walks about 2½ hours. Also close by the War Memorial is a lookout, and underneath this the **Aboriginal Gallery** ⓘ T9481 7082, www.aboriginalgallery.com.au, Mon-Fri 1030-1630, Sat-Sun 1100-1600, a workshop and gallery for local artists.

Away from the views is a large area devoted to families with young children. **Hale Oval** has an extensive, imaginative playground, several free electric BBQs with covered seating (though strangely no tables), plus a kiosk-café, **Stickybeaks** ⓘ T9481 4990, 0830-1700, with a good range of snack meals and takeaways. There are also events held at the playground, contact the café for details. Other BBQ areas are located at the Pines, off Fraser Avenue, Saw Avenue and Lakeside. The latter two picnic areas are at the west end of the park. Some BBQs, including those in the Pines, are wood-fired with wood provided free, and may be out of bounds in summer.

Northbridge and around
Across the railway line from Perth CBD, and in the same area as the Cultural Centre, visitors will find Northbridge. Best known for its restaurants, bars and clubs, it is also home to a good cinema and some interesting small specialty boutiques. Perth's **Chinatown** can be found here and there are an astonishing variety of Asian restaurants and grocers, excellent for those who are self-catering.

Northbridge has undergone urban regeneration in the last few years to make it a safer place to visit and to promote Perth as a 24-hour city. The **Northbridge Piazza**, at the corner of Lake Street and James Street, is a new community space where there is free Wi-Fi access, outdoor furniture and a big screen. Since its unveiling in 2009 the Piazza has played host to Perth's New Year celebrations, the **Summer Film Festival**, and has become a popular place for screening live sports.

Separated from the main Northbridge strip by the Cultural Centre is **Beaufort Street**, home to more nightlife and the local police station. North along here are the areas of **Highgate** and **Mount Lawley**, which are quieter but offer some good restaurants and cafés.

② Northbridge

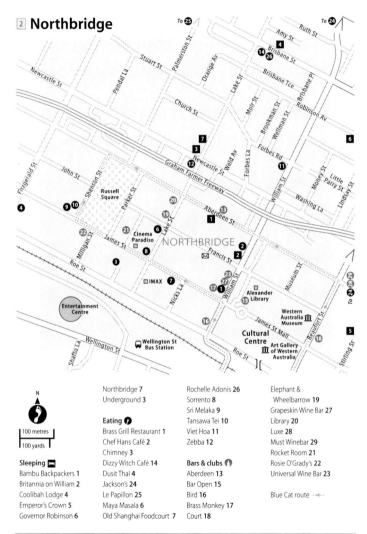

Sleeping 🛏
Bambu Backpackers **1**
Britannia on William **2**
Coolibah Lodge **4**
Emperor's Crown **5**
Governor Robinson **6**
Northbridge **7**
Underground **3**

Eating 🍴
Brass Grill Restaurant **1**
Chef Hans Café **2**
Chimney **3**
Dizzy Witch Café **14**
Dusit Thai **4**
Jackson's **24**
Le Papillon **25**
Maya Masala **6**
Old Shanghai Foodcourt **7**
Rochelle Adonis **26**
Sorrento **8**
Sri Melaka **9**
Tansawa Tei **10**
Viet Hoa **11**
Zebba **12**

Bars & clubs 🍸
Aberdeen **13**
Bar Open **15**
Bird **16**
Brass Monkey **17**
Court **18**
Elephant &
  Wheelbarrow **19**
Grapeskin Wine Bar **27**
Library **20**
Luxe **28**
Must Winebar **29**
Rocket Room **21**
Rosie O'Grady's **22**
Universal Wine Bar **23**

Blue Cat route ⤙⤙

Central suburbs

The suburbs north of the river and west of the city centre are some of the most attractive in the city. These suburbs all have their own character and most have eating and shopping strips that are more lively than the city centre.

Subiaco and around

Subiaco is a stylish eating destination, although it is more expensive than Northbridge and too trendy for some. It now has a large, busy suburban commercial strip but it had spiritual beginnings far from its current celebration of materialism. It was founded as a monastery, New Subiaco, by two homesick Italian monks who also founded the more famous monastery at New Norcia. There are two small museums here, both worth a look if you have the time. The **WA Medical Museum** ① *Harvey House, Barker St, T9340 1506, Wed 1030-1600, Sun 1400-1600, $4, children $1*, is an exhibition of the history of medicine in WA housed in Perth's first maternity hospital. The **Subiaco Museum** ① *Rokeby Rd, T9237 9227, Tue-Sun 1400-1700, gold coin donation*, displays local artefacts and memorabilia charting the history of Subi from one-time Benedictine monastery to the buzzing suburb that it is today.

Between Subiaco and the city centre, **West Perth** is mostly a professional suburb

Sleeping 🛏	Brew-Ha 3	Zen 10
Eight Nicholson 1	Buddhabar 4	
Richardson Hotel & Spa 2	Chutney Mary's 12	Bars & clubs 🍸
	Rialto's 1	Subiaco Hotel 12
Eating 🍴	Walk Café 8	
Alaturka 11	Witch's Cauldron 9	

where architects, accountants and dentists have their offices. There are also lots of apartments and it makes a very convenient base close to Kings Park, Subiaco restaurants, the city and the freeway.

Just north of Subiaco, **Leederville** is an alternative and funky suburb with some great cafés, a lively pub and an arthouse cinema with indoor and outdoor screens. The shops are all independent establishments selling books, clothing, homewares and music.

East Perth

East Perth is developing into a centre for accommodation and eating but is still fairly quiet and businesslike. It is also a convenient base, although parking can be difficult. As for sights, it is home to **WACA** ⓘ *Nelson Crescent, off Murray St, T9265 7318, www.waca. com.au, museum Mon-Fri 1000-1500 except match days, $5, children $3, ground tours Mon-Thu 1000 and 1300 except match days, $12.50, children $5, concessions $10, Red CAT route, stop 6*, (pronounced simply 'wacker'), WA's premier sporting stadium. It is now used almost exclusively for cricket and there are regular tours of the ground and a small but fascinating museum, mostly filled with a 100 years' worth of cricketing memorabilia and including a Bradman room. Head to gate two for both tours and museum.

Opposite the WACA, the **Queen's Gardens** are a picturesque set of lawns and palm trees set around a series of lily ponds, a surprisingly quiet spot. In the other direction **Gloucester Park** ⓘ *T9323 3555, www.gloucesterpark.com.au, $10, children (under 18) free, concessions $5*, is a trotting circuit that holds horse races every Monday afternoon from 1300 and Friday evenings from 1800 (gates open from 1700).

Nedlands and Claremont

Heading southwest, the Stirling Highway is an arterial route between the river and coast from the city to Fremantle, and links the leafy, establishment suburbs of Nedlands, Claremont and Cottesloe. **Nedlands** abuts the western border of the University of Western Australia (UWA), the state's oldest university with a beautiful garden campus and an excellent art gallery. **Claremont** has some great shopping and is the haunt of 'ladies who lunch'.

South Perth

Just across Perth Water, South Perth has the best city views and a lovely foreshore. This is a great place for sailing or waterskiing and there are hire outlets here during the summer. Several cafés and restaurants are located right on the riverbank and although you might pay a little more for the view, it is a pleasant place to spend a few hours. Alternatively, just head for the eastern end of the foreshore where there are also plenty of good places to picnic, BBQ and walk by the river. In South Perth, the incongruous **Old Mill** ⓘ *T9367 5788, Tue-Fri 1000-1600, Sat-Sun 1300-1600, gold coin donation, by Narrows Bridge, catch a ferry to Mends St jetty, then walk towards the bridge (10 mins) or take bus No 108 or 109 from the Busport*, tucked under the freeway, is an unusual survivor from the early days of the Swan River Settlement in the 1830s. Although the windmill looks quaint, it is technically an industrial site and one of the oldest in the state. It was built in 1835 by William Shenton to grind wheat that fed the young colony. On a windy day the mill averaged 680 kg of flour a day and its location by the river meant that the flour could easily be transported to the city. Incredibly the mill was almost lost when the freeway and Narrows bridge were built in 1955. The government planned to demolish the site to make way for the freeway but there was such public protest that the building was saved and it is now managed by the National Trust. An exhibition in the whitewashed miller's cottage explains the history of the mill.

Also in South Perth, is **Perth Zoo** ① *20 Labouchere Rd, T9474 0444, www.perthzoo.wa. gov.au, 0900-1700, $20, children under 15 $10, concessions $16-17, Transperth ferry from Barrack St jetty to Mends St jetty, then 5-min walk or catch bus No 30 or 31 from the Esplanade Bus Station.* The zoo covers just 19 ha in a block between the river and the freeway but manages to squeeze in 1300 animals in attractive natural settings. The three main habitats are the Australian Bushwalk, Asian Rainforest and African Savannah. The zoo participates in a native species breeding program, Western Shield, that aims to save the many local WA species close to extinction, releasing zoo-bred animals in to the wild. The results of this programme can be seen in the Australian Bushwalk, housing creatures such as the tiny Western Swamp Tortoise, one of the world's rarest tortoise species, and the unusual termite-eating Numbat. A highlight of the wetlands area is the horrifyingly large saltwater crocodile. This 50-year-old from Darwin is 550 kg of power and his enclosure allows visitors to see him whether he is in the water or basking in the sun. The Asian rainforest is home to elephants, monkeys and orang-utans but the most compelling creatures are the Sumatran tigers, clearly visible through a glass wall. The displays highlight their endangered status. More big cats as well as giraffes, zebra and rhinos can be seen in the African Savannah. The zoo café and shop are located near the entrance. The café menu is limited to junk food but there is also a grassy picnic and BBQ area. On a hot day remember to take a drink or change for the drink machines en route as it can be quite a walk back to the café.

Coastal suburbs

The coastal suburbs are where you'll see Perth locals at their most relaxed. Surfwear is the customary attire and although you may not want to become familiar with a surfer's feet, you will because bare feet on the street or in shops are entirely unremarkable. These suburbs are mostly residential but most have at least one great café or restaurant on the beach. Swimming is fine at all of the beaches, although there is often a steep shore break. As always in Australia, watch out for rips. If you want the reassurance of lifeguards, swim between the flags at Cottesloe, or Scarborough beaches. City Beach, Floreat and Trigg also often have lifeguards on duty at weekends in summer. Swanbourne is a nudist beach and Trigg is mostly for surfers but the rest are used by all. All west coast beaches are most pleasant in the morning before the sea breeze, known locally as the Fremantle Doctor for the relief it brings, kicks in from the south in the afternoon. Early evening is also lovely at the beach, when the sun melts into the Indian Ocean and there are often magnificent sunsets.

Cottesloe → *11 km from city centre, 7 km from Fremantle.*
Perth's most attractive and lively beach suburb, Cottesloe, is the kind of place to make anyone envy the local lifestyle, or persuade them to immigrate here as soon as possible. The blindingly white beaches of Cottesloe and North Cottesloe slope into the clear, warm water of the Indian Ocean and there is usually a bit of a swell for bodysurfing. The beaches attract a hardy band of local swimmers early in the morning who are replaced later in the day by the city's best bodies and bikinis. There are always teenage boys showing off on the pylon and walkers striding along the ocean-side path. The cafés overlooking the ocean are busy from sunrise to sunset, when the sun dips into the sea as if curtsying to Cottesloe alone. It's not

glitzy though and owes its contented, laid-back atmosphere to its happy locals who far outnumber visitors. Just inland is the shopping area of Napoleon Street, just off Stirling Highway, full of classy homeware shops catering to the residents of the surrounding suburbs.

Cottesloe to Scarborough → *Distance 12 km.*
One long, sweeping beach extends all the way from Cottesloe to Scarborough, incorporating a nudist section near the military base at **Swanbourne**. This whole stretch of coast is a favourite of surfers and windsurfers alike and swimming can be hazardous. Stick to the patrolled areas. Mid-way are two small developed enclaves, and these make two of the best spots on the Perth coast if you want to get away from the serious crowds. **City Beach** has an extensive grassy foreshore hard up against a very broad section of beautiful white-sand beach. Facilities include BBQs, picnic tables and toilets and a small complex with a kiosk, café and the best restaurant in Perth that actually hangs over a beach. See Eating, page 44, for details of the great eatery, **Oceanus**.

Just a few hundred metres north, **Floreat Beach** is much more modest in scale, but with a superb children's playground, BBQs and some unexpectedly stylish, covered picnic tables. There are also two beach volleyball courts; free, collect a ball and net from the kiosk. There is a laid-back, friendly terrace café (see Eating, page 45).

Scarborough → *14 km from city centre, 9 km from Hillarys.*
Where Cottesloe is an almost accidentally popular beach suburb, laid-back and effortless, Scarborough's attractions are more carefully designed. The suburb is dominated by the **Rendezvous Observation Tower**, a multi-storeyed icon built by Alan Bond that somehow slipped through council planning regulations in the 1980s. It is the only skyscraper on the entire city coastline. In front of it a small café strip has developed, separated from the wide beach by a road, narrow grassy foreshore and a thin line of remnant dunes. Facilities are good and family-friendly including toilets, BBQs, picnic tables, takeaway kiosks and a small cabin hiring out a variety of games, skates and bikes. Around the main junction of the West Coast Highway and Scarborough Beach Road is a cluster of shops and services, including a Coles supermarket. Beyond these are a large number of three- to four-storey holiday apartment complexes. **Scarborough Beach Markets**, held every weekend, pale besides those in the city and Fremantle, but are worth a visit for a well- stocked second-hand book stall.

Scarborough to Sorrento
A kilometre or so north of Scarborough the long sweep of beach that has extended practically all the way from Port Beach finally starts to break into a series of smaller bays and coves. The sand at this breakpoint is called **Trigg Beach**, and it is one of the city's best surfing spots. The beach backs onto large, grassy **Clarko Reserve**, where there are BBQs, covered picnic areas, toilets and changing rooms, and a children's playground. Just to the south, almost on the beach, is the **Trigg Island Café** (see Eating, page 45).

A little further north **Mettam's Pool** is one of the few beaches on the Perth coast that favours swimmers and snorkellers over surfers, due to an off-shore reef, close to the surface, that has created a sheltered 'pool'. There are toilets and changing rooms available, and a few picnic tables. Continuing north you will pass the quite average **Waterman's Beach**. Not at all average is the small, funky terrace café across the road, the BYO **Wild Fig** (see Eating, page 45).

Hillarys and Sorrento → *25 km from centre, 27 km from Swan Valley.*

The beach suburbs of Hillarys and Sorrento have put themselves well and truly on the map, particularly for families, by building **Hillarys Boat Harbour**. Primarily containing private moorings the harbour does have a few commercial operations, but has become better known for the shops, restaurants and activities on and around the mall-like **Sorrento Quay**, a pier which almost bisects the harbour and ensures a very well-protected beach. Two major family attractions means the harbour and quay really hum on a weekend and during school holidays, particularly as the harbour also protects a sandy beach.

AQWA ① *Southside Dr, T9447 7500, www.aqwa.com.au, daily 1000-1700, $28, children $16, concessions $20*, WA's premier aquarium, is an impressive showcase for the sealife that inhabits the coastal waters around the state. The centrepiece is a large walk-through tank with a good variety of fish, sharks and rays, but the many side tanks are just as fascinating with several devoted to corals and jellyfish. You'll want the Moon jellyfish tank back home in your living room. There are also discovery pools, crocodiles, a theatre showing almost continuous undersea documentaries and a large outdoor seal pool with an adjacent underground viewing room. Regular feeding and educational sessions can easily turn this into a half-day visit. A cheap café serves healthy sandwiches, cheap hot lunches, cakes and drinks.

The Great Escape ① *T9448 0800, www.thegreatescape.com.au, slides Feb-Dec 1000-1700, Dec-Jan 0900-2100, high ropes course daily 1000-1800, complex Mar-Sep 1000-1700, Oct-Feb 1000-2000*, serving as the backdrop to the harbour beach, is a no-nonsense children's attraction with several diversions clustered around the all-important water slides. These are open for three fixed three-hour sessions, so best to arrive just after the start of one of them. Unfortunately everything is priced separately so it can rack up a bit if the kids insist on trying everything. A kiosk supplies drinks and snacks.

Perth listings

For Sleeping and Eating price codes and other relevant information, see pages 10-14.

🛏 Sleeping

Central Perth *p24, map p26*

St George's and Adelaide Terraces are home to many of the big modern, glitzy hotels in Perth, all with superb balcony rooms overlooking the riverside parks and the river itself. All offer cheaper 'getaway' specials so it might be worth asking what's going.

$$$$ The Duxton, 1 St George's Terr, T9261 8000, www.duxton.com. The closest to the city centre and its rooms and services are, by a whisker, the benchmark for the rest. Facilities include Wi-Fi. The main restaurant is also good.

$$$$-$$$ Hyatt Regency, 99 Adelaide Terr, T9225 1234, www.perth.hyatt.com. The last of the clutch of international standard hotels strung out along this street. It is arranged around an impressive atrium foyer and has recently been refurbished. Wi-Fi and underground parking facilities available. Self-parking $20, valet parking $30.

$$$$-$$$ The Melbourne, corner of Hay and Milligan Sts, T9320 3333, www.melbourne hotel.com.au. Boutique hotel with 33 rooms in an ornate, restored 1890s pub building. Rooms have TV, en suite, some with veranda. Bar, café and restaurant. 24-hr reception.

$$$ Miss Maud Swedish Hotel, 97 Murray St, T9325 3900, www.missmaud.com.au. A very central hotel within easy reach of the main shopping streets and train station. The 52 rooms are standard and some of the Scandinavian decor may not be to guest's taste but it's clean and the Smörgåsbord breakfast is included in the rate (you may not have to eat again for the rest of the day). There is a restaurant but no parking.

$$$ Sullivans, 166 Mounts Bay Rd, T9321 8022, www.sullivans.com.au. Just below Kings Park, this comfortable, modern hotel has 68 rooms (some with balcony and river views) and 2 apartments. Also pool, free bikes, free internet, parking, restaurant, café and 24-hr reception. Convenient location, free city bus (Blue CAT) at door.

$$$-$$ Criterion Hotel, 560 Hay St, T9325 5155, www.criterion-hotel-perth.com.au. A glorious art deco façade does not prepare you for the interior. The hotel has been refurbished to provide 69 comfortable but bland modern rooms, all a/c with minibar. Convenient location in heart of city, also a good brasserie and pub on site. Wi-Fi but no parking.

$$ Townsend Lodge, 240 Adelaide Terr, T9325 4143, www.townsend.wa.edu.au. Mostly used for student accommodation, the friendly Townsend has 60 clean single rooms and 2 doubles on separate male and female floors. Lots of facilities including pool table, TV room, DVD hire, internet access, laundry and courtyard BBQ. Price drops by 30% for stays of 2 nights or more. Helpful staff. Reception hours 0900-1900, Sat-Sun 0900-1700.

$$-$ Perth City YHA, 300 Wellington St, T9287 3333. One of the few hostels in Perth CBD, the rooms are nothing to write home about but the facilities are good. The communal spaces and bathrooms are large and clean, and there is even a gym on site. The bar serves up cheap meals and there's car parking from $10-11.50. It is however, next to the train line so it's noisy.

Self-contained

$$$ Riverview on Mount Street, 42 Mount St, T9321 8963, www.riverviewperth.com.au. Stylish, well-equipped studio apartments, all with balconies or patio gardens. Quality with value for couples, friendly and helpful staff.

There is a restaurant next door for those who don't want to cook, it's open daily for breakfast and lunch and Tue-Sat for dinner. Recommended.

$$$-$$ Mountway, 36 Mount St, T9321 8307, www.mountwayunits.com.au. A far less glamorous high-rise block overlooking the freeway and the city. Kitchens are basic and the traffic noise can be considerable, but these self-contained units are fairly spacious. All have balconies; linen, blankets and towels are provided. Facilities include internet and laundry. Limited off-street parking available.

$$ City Waters Lodge, 118 Terrace Rd, T9325 1566, www.citywaters.com.au. Clean and comfortable studio units (58) and 2-bed apartments (3) overlooking Langley Park. Each unit has a kitchen, bathroom, TV, a/c and Wi-Fi, serviced daily. German-speaking staff, continental breakfast available. Good value.

Northbridge and around *p29, maps p26 and p30*

$$$$-$$ Northbridge Hotel, corner of Lake and Brisbane Sts, T9328 5254, www.hotelnorth bridge.com.au. Renovated old corner hotel with veranda. Luxurious hotel rooms (50) with spa and full facilities, bar and mid-range restaurant. Budget rooms in the old part of the hotel with shared facilities, TV, fridge.

$$-$ Bambu Backpackers, 75-77 Aberdeen St, T9328 1211, www.bambu.net.au. Asian-style boutique backpackers with large kitchen, internet access, Wi-Fi, free breakfast, pool table and outdoor BYO lounge. Very friendly staff. Special weekly rates and a lot of guests are long-stayers. There's a party every Fri night.

$$-$ Britannia on William, 253 William St, T9227 6000, www.perthbritannia.com. A large, clean, comfortable hostel with 160 beds, good kitchen and dining facilities. Facilities include bike and DVD hire, darts, book exchange, laundry and internet access.

24-hr reception. No parking available.

$$-$ Coolibah Lodge, 194 Brisbane St, T9328 9958, www.coolibahlodge.com.au. Hostel with 4- and 6-bed dorms in restored colonial house. Good doubles with fridge, kettle and sink in newer extension. All rooms a/c. Small but pleasant courtyard BBQ areas and good communal areas. Other facilities include licensed bar, laundry and Wi-Fi. 24-hr reception and check-in. For those who want a quieter time, head to the sister hostel **12:01 East**, which is on Hay St in East Perth.

$$-$ The Emperor's Crown, 85 Stirling St, T9227 1400, www.emperorscrown.com.au. Friendly hostel with dorms (maximum 5-bed), twins, triples and en suite doubles (these have fridge, kettle and tea and coffee). Away from the main hubbub of Northbridge but just around the corner from the CAT bus stop. Pricey for a hostel and there's no breakfast included, but the rooms are clean, the communal spaces are large and bright and there is a café just next door. Luggage storage is also available. Recommended.

$$-$ Governor Robinson, 7 Robinson Av, T9328 3200, www.govrobinsons.com.au. This boutique hostel occupies a couple of 100-year-old cottages and a sympathetic extension in a very quiet street, 10-min walk from the centre. Small, but the central room and kitchen have the look and feel of a private home, not a hostel. Fresh, light rooms and linen, backpack-sized lockers, jarrah floorboards and classy bathrooms. Doubles, some with en suite, are of hotel standard. No pick-ups, street parking.

$$-$ Underground, 268 Newcastle St, T9228 3755. Massive central hostel with swimming pool, bar, well-equipped kitchen and spacious internet and guest area. Breakfast available. 4- to 10-bed dorms, all the same price. No BYO, fully licensed, free drink on arrival. 24-hr reception. Parking and internet available. Recommended.

Subiaco and around *p31, map p31*

$$$$ The Richardson Hotel & Spa, 32 Richardson St, West Perth, T9217 8888, www.therichardson.com.au. A luxury boutique hotel with 74 rooms and suites, most with balconies. Facilities include internet access, valet parking and access to the Spa. The **Opus Restaurant** is open for dinner and there is a cocktail bar.

$$$ Eight Nicholson, 8 Nicholson Rd, Subiaco, T9382 1881, www.8nicholson.com.au. Boutique luxury B&B in an historic Subiaco house. The beds are huge and the decor contemporary. Guests (there are 4 rooms) have their own entrance and breakfast can be enjoyed in the sunshine.

East Perth *p32, map p26*

$$$$-$$$ Novotel Langley, 221 Adelaide Terr, T9221 1200, www.novotelperthlangley.com.au. Opposite the **Sheraton**, does a commendable job at offering a similar experience at a slightly cheaper price. Parking.

$$ Perth City, 200 Hay St, T9220 7000, www.comforthotelperthcity.com.au. Staff are friendly, furnishings bright and cheerful. Wheelchair access, internet, 24-hr reception.

$ Exclusive Backpackers, 156 Adelaide Terr, T9221 9991, www.exclusivebackpackers. com. 25 good-quality rooms, particularly the doubles. Quiet communal areas are homely and characterful, kitchen basic. Internet and laundry facilities, reception closes at 2230.

Self-contained

$$$ The Alderney, 193 Hay St, T9225 6600, www.alderney.com.au. Has 80 very comfortably furnished, fully self-contained apartments. Indoor pool and gym and undercover parking are included. Reception hours Mon-Fri 0800-1900, Sat-Sun 0900-1500.

Nedlands *p32*

$$$ Caesia House, 32 Thomas St, T9389 8174, www.caesiahouse.com. B&B in comfortable modern house. Excellent breakfast and very knowledgeable hosts, particularly on nearby Kings Park and its flora. Also offers a self- contained apartment. Non-smoking, unsuitable for children.

Cottesloe *p33*

$$$ Cottesloe Beach Hotel, 104 Marine Terr, T9383 1100, www.cottesloebeach hotel.com.au. Comfortable art deco hotel with 13 small rooms and standard facilities. The best rooms (6) face the ocean and have a small balcony. Note that rooms are above a very popular and noisy pub. The price includes breakfast in the café. Reception opens 0800-1700.

$$$-$$ Ocean Beach Hotel, corner of Marine Parade and Eric St, T9384 2555, www.obh.com.au. Elegant rooms, some with ocean views, in a high rise opposite the beach and next to OBH bars and restaurant.

$$-$ Ocean Beach Backpackers, 1 Eric St, T9384 5111, www.oceanbeachbackpackers. com.au. This hostel is all about location, North Cott beach lies just over the road. There are dorms, twins and doubles on offer and all are en suite. Facilities include bike hire free surfboard and bodyboard hire, an in-house café, internet access, TV lounges and an XBox.

Self-contained

$$$ Cottesloe Beach Chalets, 6 John St, T9383 5000, www.cottesloebeachchalets.com.au. A complex of 30 modern self-contained flats close to the beach that sleep 5. Full kitchen, bathroom, and 2 bedrooms on mezzanine level. The complex also has a pool and BBQs. Off-street parking. Price covers 1-5 people.

Scarborough *p34*

$$$$-$$$ Hotel Rendezvous, 33 The Esplanade, Scarborough, T9340 5555, www.rendezvous hotels.com. The majority part of the Rendezvous Observation Tower, is Perth's premier non-city centre hotel. It has striking views up and down the coast and facilities include 2 restaurants, café, heated outdoor pool with spa, gym, Wi-Fi, tennis courts, 24-hr reception and room service. Parking.

$$$$-$$$ Sunmoon, 200 West Coast Highway, T9245 8000, www.sunmoon.com.au. Striking resort-style complex, with a faintly Asian feel and a wide range of hotel rooms and self-contained apartments. Hotel rates include a cooked breakfast. Wi-Fi and on-site parking available.

$$-$ Perth Beach YHA, 256 West Coast Highway, T9245 3388, www.indigonet.com.au. A 5-min walk from the Esplanade, this unpretentious hostel has 60 beds in a variety of singles, doubles, 4- and 6-bed dorms. The reception area doubles as an expensive internet café and they also offer bike and board hire. Other facilities include a garden area with BBQ.

Self-contained

$$$$-$$$ Sandcastles and **Seashells**, 170-178 The Esplanade, T9341 6644, www.seashells.com.au. 2 large resort complexes with 2-3 bedroom self-contained apartments and some motel-style rooms. Most rooms have balcony views though there is a lot of car park between the resorts and the beach. All rooms have fully equipped kitchen and laundry facilities, TV, internet access and a/c. General facilities include BBQ area and 2 outdoor swimming pools.

Hillarys and Sorrento *p35*

$$$$-$$$ Hillarys Harbour Resort Apartments, 68 Southside Dr, Hillarys, T9262 7888, www.hillarysresort.com.au. Well furnished, comfortable and modern 1- to 3-bedroom fully self-contained apartments. Most have private balconies or courtyards overlooking either the harbour or the courtyard pool. Facilities include BBQ area, heated spa and sauna. Underground parking.

Caravan and tourist parks
$$$-$$ Kingsway Tourist Park, corner of Kingsway and Wanneroo Rd, T9409 9267, www.acclaimparks.com.au. Tourist park with chalets, smaller cabins and powered sites.
$$-$ Cherokee Village, 10 Hocking Rd, T9409 9039, www.istnet.net.au/~cherokee. Self-contained cabins, some en suite. Free gas BBQ and pool. No pets allowed.

Airport
$$$-$ Perth International, T9453 6677, www.perthinternational.com.au. A Big4 caravan park with self-contained chalets and cabins. These are well-equipped and comfortable, some with spas, others with the budget conscious in mind. The grounds are immaculate, the facilities excellent, and nothing is too much trouble for the staff. Recommended.

🍽 Eating

Eating in Perth is characterized by location rather than cuisine; it is overwhelmingly an outdoor scene that makes the most of a stable, sunny climate. Many restaurants have very little indoor space and every eating area is crammed with pavement tables or open terraces. Despite Perth's isolation, the food is fresh and varied as it is mostly grown or harvested within the state. Seafood is very good and Asian or Italian food introduced by migrants is very popular. As in the other Australian states most fine restaurants make the best of both produce and flavour with a typically Modern Australian fusion of Eastern and Western cuisine.

Central Perth *p24, map p26*
There are several food courts in the city that are cheap but can be dim, messy and crowded. There is a good one upstairs in the City Arcade with an outdoor terrace overlooking Murray St Mall. Also try the

Carillion Arcade.
$$$ 1907 Bar & Restaurant, 26 Queens St, T9436 0233, www.1907.com.au. Lunch Tue-Fri 1200-1500, dinner Tue-Sat 1800-2100. Bar Wed-Thu 1700-2400, Fri-Sat 1700-0100. Housed in a 100-year-old factory in Perth's former fashion district, this is a romantic, atmospheric place serving excellent food. Opulent in its decor, the dishes are classics and for those who can't decide what to choose there's a tasting menu (Prestige). If finances can't stretch to dinner, there's a bar downstairs offering delicious cocktails.
$$$ Balthazar, 6 The Esplanade, T9421 1206. Mon-Fri 1200-1500, Mon-Sat 1800-2200. Indulgent wine bar and restaurant that cleverly combines the traditional crisp lines of folded white table linen with the even crisper lines of the metal and wood architecture. Mediterranean-influenced food is matched by the music and supported by an extensive wine list. There's a cheap bar menu for those with shallower pockets and they dig into the cellars to hold wine-tastings every 4-6 weeks.
$$$ Fraser's, Fraser Av, T9481 7100, www.frasersrestaurant.com.au. Breakfast on Sun from 0800, lunch daily from 1200, dinner daily from 1800. Has for years been one of the city's best in terms of both food, location and ambience. The view of the city is slightly obscured by trees, but it's still pretty impressive and there are a few terrace tables to make the most of it. Cuisine is Modern Australian, predominantly seafood, with a few grills, and it's supported by an extensive, quality wine list. The attached **Botanical Café** (T9482 0122) is open daily 0700-2200, and offers slightly cheaper, good-quality food.
$$$ Old Swan Brewery, 173 Mounts Bay Rd, T9211 8999, www.theoldbrewery.com.au. Daily 0730-2200. Contemporary space with lots of black furniture and a warehouse feel, with a wide terrace on the river. Modern Australian food with an emphasis on grills, including native meats.
$$ Andaluz Bar & Tapas, Basement, 21

Howard St, T9481 0092, www.andaluzbar.com.au. Mon-Thu 1200-2400, Fri 1200-0100, Sat 1800-0100. A bar serving good Spanish tapas. It has a very extensive cocktail menu to complement the wines and the digestifs. Visit in the week when it's not too busy.

$$ Barre, 825 Hay St, next door to His Majesty's Theatre, T9226 1006. Lunch only Mon-Fri, dinner when performances are running next door. A refined and elegant café with dark wood fittings. The menu is less formal, with glammed-up burgers, pizzas, salads and pasta.

$$ Café Bocca, Shafto Lane, 872 Hay St, T9226 4030. Mon-Thu 0730-1530, Fri 0730-2200. Stylish, contemporary Italian in a lovely shady courtyard by a tranquil fountain. Most tables are outdoors.

$ Annalakshmi, Jetty 4, Barrack St, T9221 3003, www.annalakshmi.com.au. Tue-Sun 1200-1400, Tue-Sun 1830-2100, closed Sat for lunch. Friendly Indian vegetarian buffet where all profits go to food and arts charities. There is no set price – you simply pay what you feel you can afford. They also put on monthly displays of Indian dancing, usually on the Sat closest to the full moon. No alcohol allowed. Booking advised.

$ Arirang, 91 Barrack St, T9225 4855, www.arirang.com.au. Daily 1130-1500, Sun-Thu 1730-2130, Fri-Sat 1730-2200. Unusual Korean BBQ restaurant with a stylish, contemporary interior. Charcoals are brought to the table for you to cook your own meat in a central well to combine with rice and sauces. Good fun with a focus on the best fresh food and Korean culture. Dinner is in the mid-range price bracket.

$ Hans, 24 Forrest Chase, T9228 8151. Daily 1100-2100. Chain of casual restaurants, always packed for their good value Thai, Japanese and Chinese dishes. Licensed.

$ Jaws, Hay St Mall. Mon-Thu 1130-1900, Fri-Sat 1130-2100, Sun 1130-1800. A true sushi bar with seats in a horseshoe facing the very cheap dishes whizzing past on the conveyor belt. Always a busy lunch spot for office workers.

$ Jaws Mint, corner of Hay St and Hill St, T9225 4573. Mon-Fri 1100-1500, 1800-2130. Principally a Japanese takeaway but has eat-in tables.

$ Matsuri, 250 St Georges Terr, T9322 7737, www.matsuri.com.au. Mon-Fri 1200-1430, Mon-Sat 1800-2200. Sushi takeaway bar on the QV1 Plaza. Good-value set menus.

Cafés

Many cafés stay open later on Fri night.

Bocelli's Espresso, a large bustling outdoor café in the heart of Forrest Pl. Daily until 1800 (until 2100 on Fri). A good place for a casual bite while watching the crowds. Gourmet sandwiches, cakes, drinks, also breakfasts.

E Cucina, 777 Hay St, next to City Park. Smart Italian food and, around the corner, a straight- up espresso bar for city workers on the run.

Merchant Tea and Coffee Company, 183 Murray St Mall (and others). Mon-Sat 0700-1900, Sun 0900-1900. An elegant respite from the mall, lined with dark wood and with cool high ceilings. Sandwiches, cakes and coffee ordered at the counter. Also pavement tables.

Tiger Tiger Coffee Bar, 4/329 Murray St, T9322 8055, www.tigertigercoffeebar.com. Mon-Wed 0700-2000, Thu-Sat 0700-2200. Good range of coffee and all-day food and breakfast. Free Wi-Fi available.

Velvet Espresso, 5/172 St Georges Terr, T9322 5209. Mon-Fri 0630-1600. A stylish but relaxed little café with 5 Senses coffee and fresh friand pastries baked by the owner.

Northbridge and around *p29, maps p26 and p30*

The **Old Shanghai** foodcourt on James St has a good range of Asian stalls. Mon-Thu 1100-2200, Fri-Sun 1100-2300.

$$$ Jackson's, 483 Beaufort St, Highgate,

T9328 1177, www.jacksonsrestaurant.com.au. Mon-Sat 1900-late. One of Perth's finest, enjoy Neal Jackson's international menu in this award-winning restaurant. Treat yourself with a 9-course tasting ('The Dego') and a glass of wine from the impressive wine list.

$$$-$$ Brass Grill Restaurant, corner of William and James Sts, T9227 9596, www.the brassmonkey.com.au. Tue-Sat 1800-late Fri for lunch 1200-1430. This brasserie on the balcony is one of the most pleasant places to dine in Northbridge. The Modern Australian menu changes regularly to reflect the use of fresh seasonal produce. Recommended.

$$$-$$ The Chimney, 171 James St, opposite Cinema Paradiso, T9328 6870. A friendly, stylish restaurant serving modern Australia and Italian meals. There is also a good wine list. Outdoor seating is available in the courtyard. Recommended.

$$$-$$ Dusit Thai, 249 James St, T9328 7647, www.dusitthai.com.au. Tue-Sun 1800-2200. Award-winning, elegant and ornate Thai serving consistently fresh and creative food. Licensed and BYO. Takeaway also available. Runs cooking classes.

$$$-$ Sorrento Restaurant, 158 James St, T9328 7461, www.sorrentorestaurant.com.au. This popular Italian serves good-value pizzas and a decent range of Mediterranean dishes. Fully licensed, BYO Mon-Thu.

$$ Chef Han's Café, 245 William St, T93228 8122 and T9328 8119, www.hanscafe.com.au. Daily 1100-2200. Very busy large noodle bar with most dishes around $10-12. Flavour makes up for very bland surroundings.

$$ Tansawa Tei, 1 Shenton St, T9228 0258. Tue-Sat 1130-1430, 1800-2230. Elegant and contemporary Japanese overlooking the park. Set menus are good value for the whole culinary experience but lunch or a light meal can be had for under $20.

$ Maya Masala, corner of Lake St and Francis St, T9328 5655. Daily 1130-late. Wonderful Indian food in groovy, contemporary style.

Specialities are dosa, thali, curries and tandoori but also particularly perfect Indian sweets. Prices are almost too good to be true. Licensed and BYO. Recommended.

$ Sri Melaka, 220 James St, T228 2882 and T9328 6404, www.yongcorp.com.au. Tue-Sun 1130-1530, 1730-2130. Buffet or à la carte veggie versions of Chinese, Indian and Malaysian favourites. Also a good range of salads, tasty desserts and non-alcoholic drinks. The surroundings are fairly simple but it's good-value food with friendly service. Vegetarian market next door.

$ Viet Hoa, 349 William St, T9328 2127. Daily 1000-2200. Vietnamese and Chinese food served in this large, businesslike restaurant. Always very busy and great value. Most dishes are under $15. Not licensed, BYO. Takeaway available.

Cafés

The Dizzy Witch Café, 197 Brisbane St, T9228 1501, www.thedizzywitchcafe.com.au. Tue-Sun 0700-1600. Offers a good and varied breakfast menu, as well as hearty lunch options. Cakes and coffees, and free Wi-Fi.

Le Papillon, 274 Bulwer St, Highgate, T9227 6664. Mon-Fri 0700-1600, Sat-Sun 0700-1700. A little out of the way but the coffee and patisseries are worth the trip. A good place for breakfast, lunch or just a cup of tea and a cake, it has a nice French vibe to it. The outside tables are next to a busy road.

Rochelle Adonis, 193 Brisbane St, T9227 0007, www.rochelleadonis.com.au. Tue-Sat 1000-1600. Cakes and confections, think delicate cupcakes and strawberry tarts.

Zebba, 101 Lake St, T9228 4029. Mon-Fri 0700-1700 and Sat 0800-1400. A hole-in-the-wall café serving good coffee and simple but filling food.

Subiaco and around p31, map p31
Subiaco is fast becoming central Perth's social hub. Rokeby Rd, between Bagot and Roberts Sts, is the main strip, with several

good options along Hay St.

$$$ Rialto's, 424 Hay St, T9382 3292, www.rialtos.com.au. Wed-Fri 1200-late, Tue and Sat 1800-late. Large dining room suited to the serious business of eating award-winning top-quality cuisine. The menu is tight on choice, but supported by a considerable wine list.

$$$ Witch's Cauldron, 89 Rokeby Rd, T9381 2508, www.witchs.com.au. Daily 0730-1100, 1200-2130, weekends until 2230. Formal restaurant with a traditional feel only slightly off-set by pictures of pointy-hatted ladies. Cuisine is Modern Australian and dependably good. Mostly seafood, chicken and steak grills with a few veggie options.

$$$-$ Alaturka, 420 Hay St, T9388 9029, www.alaturka.com.au. Daily 0930-2200. A friendly Turkish restaurant in modern surrounds. Staff are very helpful and are happy to offer suggestions if guests are new to Turkish cuisine. Licensed and BYO. Takeaway available.

$$ Buddhabar, 88 Rokeby Rd, T9382 2941, www.buddhabar.com.au. Fri-Sat 1200-1430, Tue-Sun 1800-late. Hip Indian that puts as much creativity into its music and surrounds as its curries. Relaxed and friendly, their late night 'supper clubs' give a whole new cultured meaning to a late-night curry. Licensed, live music Tue-Sat.

$$-$ Chutney Mary's, corner of Hay St and Rokeby St, T9381 2099, www.chutney marys.com.au. Open Mon-Sat for lunch and daily for dinner from 1730. A popular Indian restaurant, book ahead if coming on Fri or Sat night when it can be very noisy. The menu has a wide variety of options and the lunch specials are good value. Fully licensed.

$ Zen, 1 Seddon St, T9381 4931, www.zen-perth.com. Tue-Fri 1200-1400, Tue-Sat 1800-2200, Sun 1800-2100. Traditional, licensed Japanese with seriously cheap takeaway lunch specials. BYO.

Cafés

There are several good cafés in Subiaco and they can all be relied upon for a decent coffee. The 2 below are located on pedestrian walk-throughs, and so have the appeal of larger outdoor areas that are away from road traffic.

Brew-Ha, 162 Rokeby Rd, T9388 7272, www.brew-ha.com.au. Open 0630-1800. Fresh coffee and tea, by the packet or the cup. Comfy chairs and laid-back style make this a good spot to enjoy the morning paper.

Walk Café, Forrest Walk. Open 0730-1530. Cool, contemporary and relaxed with plenty of outside tables. Light lunches come in big servings.

Leederville *p32*

This inner-city suburb has developed a small café scene around the junction of Oxford and Newcastle Sts. At its heart is the arthouse **Luna Cinema**. The **Leederville** pub is also a big draw for the area.

$$$-$$ Kailis Bros Fish Café, 101 Oxford St, T9443 6300, www.kailisbrosleederville. com.au. Daily 0830-2130. An unusual but elegant seafood restaurant that shares an open space with a fresh fish market. You can even select seafood to be cooked for you. Every kind of fish and seafood, Greek mezze plates, dips and wonderful seafood platters. Also takeaways and breakfast.

$$ Giardini, 135 Oxford St, T9242 2602, www.giardini.com.au. Daily 0730-late. Sophisticated Italian with good service and a modern twist to the cooking. Large, relaxing space has cane chairs and lots of greenery.

$ Banzai, 741 Newcastle St, T9227 7990. Mon-Sat 1800-2130. A slick modern sushi and noodle bar. Also has internet access. Licensed and BYO.

$ Hawkers Hut, 150 Oxford, T9444 6662. Open daily for lunch and dinner. Asian food under $10.

Cafés

Greens & Co, 123 Oxford St, T9444 4093. 0630-2400. The doors open out onto the street and invite patrons in for a cup of coffee and a huge slab of cake. Rolls are available for lunch. Paper lanterns hang from the ceilings and the walls are covered in posters. The clientele is a nice mix of families, students and tourists all relaxing on the comfy sofas.

East Perth *p32, map p26*
$$ Han Palace, 73 Bennett St, T9325 8883. Tue-Thu 1200-1500, 1800-2200, Fri 1200-1500, 1800-2200, Sat 1800-2300, Sun 1800-2130. A traditional Chinese with a very regal dining room. The food is very good and you can eat cheaply. Fully licensed.
$ Mai's, 51 Bennett St, T9325 6206. Mon, Wed-Fri 1130-1430 and 1730-2230, Sat-Sun 1700-2200. A decidedly unsexy, traditional Vietnamese with a much more attractive cheap menu. BYO.

Cafés

Epic Espresso, 5/1297 Hay St (entrance on Outram St), T9485 1818, www.epicespresso.com.au. Mon-Fri 0630-1600. Serves seriously good gourmet coffees plus heavenly Belgian and French hot chocolates for non-coffee drinkers. It also offers barista workshops.

Claremont *p32*
Most of the eating options in Claremont can be found in a small area around Bay View Terr and Stirling Highway.
$$$ On the Terrace, 37 Bay View Terr, T9284 5400, www.ontheterrace.com.au. Mon-Sat 0800-late, Sun 0800-1600. The outdoor terrace is the place to be seen in this very sophisticated, fashionable restaurant and bar. Pizzas, salads, pasta and an inventive tapas menu. The bar serves a good range of cocktails at night. DJs on Thu until 0200, live jazz on Fri and Sat evenings. Champagne breakfast on Sun.
$$ Pronto, 16 Bay View Terr, T9284 6090.

Tue-Sat 0730-2230. Always buzzing for its clever combination of effusive, charming service, colourful smart room and good-value pizzas and pasta.
$$ Rudy's, 3 Bay View Terr, T9385 5282. Mon-Sat 1000-2200. Another Italian eatery serving good pizzas, pastas and salads, Takeaway available.

Nedlands *p32*
Nedlands is more spread out but there are some good places only a short distance from public transport.
$$$-$$ Jojo's Café, Broadway Jetty, T9386 8757, www.jojosrestaurant.com. Tue-Sat 1130-late, Sun to 1600, closed for breakfast during Nov-Jan. Fine water-view restaurants with boardwalk tables and a good range of light and seafood dishes.
$$ Pata Negra, 26 Stirling Highway, T9389 5517, www.patanegra.com.au. Fri 1200-1500, Tue-Sat 1700-late. A tapas bar, combining Spanish and Middle Eastern influences. Good range of beers and wines. It can, however, be noisy when it gets busy.
$ Hot Box, 38 Broadway, T9386 6600. For takeaways, fresh noodles, rice, curries, pasta $10-15.

Cafés

Barrett's Bread, 19A Broadway, T9389 6404. Mon-Fri 0630-1730, Sat and Sun 0630-1530. Bakery café with an awesome selection of French and Italian breads and pastries. Great place for a quick coffee and cake or picnic supplies.

South Perth *p32*
With a million-dollar view over Perth Water to the city, you'd expect a host of restaurants and cafés to enjoy it from, but there are only a handful. **Boatshed's** view is the best, and the **Bookcaffé** doesn't have one.
$$$ Boatshed Café, Coode St Jetty, T9474 1314, www.boatshedrestaurant.com. Mon-Fri 0730-2200, Sat and Fri 0800-2200. On the

river foreshore facing the city skyline, this airy, open restaurant is smart but unfussy. Modern Australian food that steals flavours from every major world cuisine. Fully licensed. Also has a cheap kiosk (open 0700-2000) on one side selling drinks, fish and chips, scones and muffins, with outdoor tables so the impecunious can also enjoy the view.

$$$ Coco's, corner of South Perth Esplanade and Mends St, T9474 3030, www.westvalley. com.au. Daily 0800-late. One of Perth's swankiest establishments, specializing in seafood and grills. Frequently changing menus. Specials depend on what's looking best at the markets.

$$ Bellhouse, Mends St Jetty, T9367 1699. Daily 0700-2300. Warm upmarket food café with lots of golden wood fittings, perched at the end of the jetty. The menu is mostly seafood, with a few snack options, also breakfast at the weekends.

Cafés
Mill Point Caffé Bookshop, 254 Mill Point Rd, T9367 4567. Daily 0830-1730. Sells a good range of new books that you can purchase then read to your heart's content over a coffee or a light meal.

Cottesloe p33
Most of the mid-range restaurants are cheap for lunch.

$$$ Indiana, 99 Marine Parade, T9385 5005, www.indiana.com.au. Daily 1200-1530, 1800-late. This mansion above the surf club and Cottesloe Beach is a colonial-style restaurant with echoes of the Raj in its cane armchairs and fine linen. The food, mostly seafood, is very good and the ocean views magnificent but this is one of the most expensive restaurants in the city. Very pleasant for afternoon tea.

$$$-$$ Blue Duck, 151 Marine Parade, T9385 2499, www.blueduck.com.au. Daily 0630-2100. A long-standing Cottesloe favourite, the café hangs above the beach

with mesmerizing views. Particularly good for breakfast, light lunches include wood-fired pizzas and pasta, more emphasis on fish and seafood for dinner. Takeaway fish and chips available 1200-2100. Recommended.

$$$-$$ VanS, 1 Napoleon St, T9384 0696. Daily 0700-late. A classy but casual café with sophisticated sandwiches, salads and platters to share. Simple pasta and seafood dishes that let the quality of the ingredients shine.

$$$-$ Blue Waters, 110 Marine Parade, T9385 3130, www.blue-waters.com.au. Mon-Sat 0800-late and Sun 0800-1500. Open for breakfast, lunch and dinner and offering a wide range of interesting options using fresh and often local ingredients.

$$ Ogdens Bar and Grill, Albion Hotel, T9383 0021. Daily 1200-1430, Mon-Wed, Sun 1800-2100, Thu-Sat 1800-2200. A smart 'cook your own' grill with a good selection of salads and other accompaniments. A small section of the dining room is inside an old tram, which also provides part of the outer wall.

$$-$ Barista, 38 Napoleon St, T9383 3545. Daily 0600-1700. Funky café offering burgers, sandwiches and cakes. Licensed.

$ Amberjacks Fish Café, corner of Marine and John St, T9385 0977. Daily 1100-2000. Head here for fish and chips on the beach.

$ Beaches, 122 Marine Parade, T9384 4412. Daily 0630-1600. Always busy, most of this café's seating is arranged under a shaded terrace next to a Norfolk pine. Breakfast menu served all day.

Cottesloe to Scarborough p34
$$$-$$ Oceanus, 195 Challenger Parade, City Beach, T9385 7555, www.oceanus.com.au. Tue-Sat 1200-1500, 1800-late, Sun 0800- 1700. Has a large wood-beamed dining room with floor-to-ceiling windows overlooking the ocean. Most seating is indoor with a few tables on a small balcony to the side. The expensive fusion cuisine is excellent and the

service friendly and attentive. The upper floor houses a showcase gallery for WA artists. Mezze, snacks and coffee available in the **Oceanus Café** daily 0800-1600.

$$ Costa Azzurra, Floreat Av, Floreat Beach, T9285 0048. Serves a good range of light Mediterranean meals daily from 0700-2200 in summer, 0900-2100 in winter. The café is beachside with tables overlooking the ocean. BYO.

Scarborough *p34*
$$$-$$ Zanders, 1 Scarborough Beach Rd, T9245 2001, www.zanders.com.au. Daily 0700- late. This corner restaurant serves excellent European cuisine, has friendly service and is a prime spot to watch Scarborough's busy Esplanade. Also takeaways.

$$ Jimmy Dean's, 2nd floor, Esplanade, corner of Manning St, T9205 1271, www.jimmydeansdiner.com. Daily 1200-late. Friendly American diner with a range of quality grills and cheap burgers, some good-value mid-week lunch specials. Some balcony tables have good ocean views.

$ Peters by the Sea, 128 Esplanade, T9341 1738. Open from 0900 to past midnight. A takeaway and the automatic choice for locals. They serve up excellent fish and chips, kebabs and souvlaki, and even provide covered terrace tables.

Scarborough to Sorrento *p34*
$$$-$$ Wild Fig Café, 33 West Coast Dr, Waterman's Beach, T9246 9222, www.wildfig.com.au. Daily 0630-late. Relaxed, people- and eco-friendly and the staff donate all tips and corkage to charity. It serves lots of tasty snacks and salads, juices and smoothies, and has live music Tue-Fri and Sun nights. Tue is curry and Wed vego night. Licensed and BYO. Also takeaway and free Wi-Fi. Recommended.

$$ Trigg Island Café, 360 West Coast Dr, Trigg Beach, T9447 0077, www.triggisland

cafe.com.au. Daily from 0830, main meals from 1200 and dinner from 1800, weekend breakfast 0800-1030. A large, sunny and very popular place with a beachside terrace. Dependably good, light mid-range meals include pastas, salads, seafood and grills.

Hillarys and Sorrento *p35*
$$$ Portofinos, Hillarys Boat Harbour, Southside Dr, T9246 4700, www.porto finos.com.au. Mon-Sat 1100-2100, Sun from 0800. Stylish Italian restaurant with a Romanesque interior and large covered terrace. Extensive menu includes pasta, oysters, salads and wood-fired pizzas, plus breakfast on Sun.

$$ Jetty's, Sorrento Quay, T9448 9066, www.jettys.com.au. Open 0700-1030, 1200-1530, 1730-2200. Large smorgasbord affair with good food at reasonable prices. Seafood is always on a menu that changes its theme each month. Café area open all day.

$$-$ Spinnakers, 95 Northside Dr, T9203 5266, www.spinnakerscafe.com.au. Sun-Tue 0800-1700, Wed-Sat 0800-2300. Ploughs its lone furrow on the 'opposite' side of the harbour to all the rest. Its great position is enhanced by friendly service, fresh simple meals and a bright decor. The few covered tables on the outside decking are the ones to go for. BYO only. It serves delicious banana pancakes and more for breakfast, coffee and terrific cakes until 1730. Recommended.

🎵 Bars and clubs

Central Perth *p24, map p26*
See the website www.teknoscape.com.au, for details of club nights and events.

Belgian Beer Café Westende, corner of Murray and King Sts, T9321 4094, www.belgianbeer.com.au. Meals Sun-Thu 1200-2130, Fri-Sat 1200-2200. Mon-Tue 1100-2300, Wed-Sat 1100-2400 and Sun 1100-2200. As you'd expect, Belgian beer on tap and good selection in the fridge. Serves pub food and bar snacks, also does specials such as Oyster Hour. Spacious wooden interior and pavement tables. Sat and Thu live music, burlesque dancing first Fri of the month.

Durty Nelly's Irish Pub, Shafto Lane, T9226 0233, www.durtynellys.com.au. Irish pub with a dark, cosy interior enriched by a large outdoor terrace on the lane. Irish dishes and Australian pub food Mon-Sat 1130-2100, Sun 1200-2000. Lunch specials available. Live music on Fri and Sat night, and Sun during the day.

The George, 216 St George's Terr, T6161 6662, www.thegeorgeperth.com.au. Mon-Fri 0700-2400, Sat 1700-2400. A tavern that offers restaurant standard food. Breakfast, nibbles and hearty mains, the dishes vary from pub favourites to more sophisticated fare. The cocktails are very good and the wine list comprehensive. It gets busy at weekends, so if coming for food arrive early.

Greenhouse, 100 St Georges Terr, T9481 8333, www.greenhouseperth.com. Mon-Sat 0700- late. Visitors can't miss this establishment with its outside walls covered in terracotta potted strawberry plants. Inside, the insulation is straw, the furniture is recycled timber and booze bottles are artistically hung from ropes above the bar. There is a restaurant and bar downstairs serving seasonal fare, and a separate bar upstairs surrounded by a garden growing ingredients for the kitchen. Live music on Sat nights. Good cocktails.

Grosvenor Hotel, corner of Hay and Hill Sts, near the Perth Mint, T9325 3799, www.thegrosvenorperth.com.au. Mon-Sat 1100-2400, Sun 1100-2200. Has a large outdoor terrace, well shaded and with lots of tables. A contemporary, stylish feel has been grafted into this old pub, but the menu combines traditional counter meals with a few spicy snacks available Mon-Fri 1200-1500 and 1600-2100, Sat-Sun 1200-2100.

Helvetica, near 101 St George's Terr (laneway off Howard St), T9321 4422,

www.helvetica bar.com. Tue-Thu 1500-1200, Fri 1200-1200, Sat 1800-1200. A stylish place hidden amongst the tower blocks. See the blackboard behind the bar the newest drinks, or lose yourself in the whisk(e)y menu. There are cocktails, beers and a good wine list as well as tasty bar snacks. Free Wi-Fi.

Hula Bula Bar, 12 Victoria Av, T9225 4457, www.hulabulabar.com. Wed-Fri 1600-late, Sat 1800-late. This funky Tiki cocktail bar serves inventive drinks in creative mugs. Groovy 1950s-1970s music, relaxed atmosphere. Recommended.

Moon and Sixpence, 300 Murray St. Very British, popular with those wanting a drink in the sun. More than 15 beers on tap.

Tiger Lil's, 437 Murray St, T9322 7377, www.tigerlils.com.au. Tue-Sat from 1200. This Asian pub offers a mix of authentic shared dishes, creative cocktails, international beers and DJ music in an oriental setting.

Northbridge and around *p29, maps p26 and p30*

Aberdeen, 84 Aberdeen St, T9227 9361, www.thedeen.com. Mon and Sat 1800-0200, Thu-Fri 1700-0200. A huge venue popular with students and backpackers, especially on Mon night when there are drink specials and DJs. Thu is Latin Beats.

Bar Open, 232-234 William St, T9227 0106. Wed-Thu 2000-0300, Fri-Sat 2000-0600. One of Perth's hidden secrets, this club can only be reached via a back alley. It is small but popular among those in the know. DJ music.

The Bird, 181 William St, www.william streetbird.com. This music venue hosts a range of live bands and has an alternative vibe. It's small so arrive early or you'll n ever get to the bar. Check the website to find out what's on.

The Brass Monkey, 209 William St, T9227 9596, www.thebrassmonkey.com.au. Mon-Tue 1100-2400, Wed-Thu 1100-0100, Fri-Sat 1100-0200, Sun 1100-2200. Northbridge's distinctive landmark, built in

1897. Mellow old front bar, quiet courtyard seats and the Tap Room for serious beer drinkers and sports watchers. Excellent brasserie upstairs (see Eating, page 41), sophisticated wine bar next door.

The Court, 50 Beaufort St, T9328 5292, www.thecourt.com.au. Gay venue with DJs, drag shows and live bands. Also pool tables, bar snacks and a beer garden.

Elephant and Wheelbarrow, 53 Lake St, T9228 4433, www.elephantandwheelbarrow. com.au. Mon-Thu 1100-2400, Fri-Sat 1200-0300, Sun 1200-2400. British-style pub popular with backpackers. British and Irish beers on tap and in bottles, live covers and retro music Wed-Sun, cheap pub grub and pleasant shady terrace.

Grapeskin Wine Bar, 209 William St, T9227 9596. Bar Mon-Tue 1200-2400, Wed-Thu 1200-0100, Fri-Sat 1200-0200, Sun 1200-2200. Stylish, contemporary bar and bottleshop attracts a sophisticated crowd of beautiful people. Also has good menu of grazing and sharing food available 1200-2200. Shares food specials with **The Brass Monkey** next door.

Library, 69 Lake St, T9328 1065, www.librarynightclub.com.au. Open 2000-late. DJs entertain clubbers in the 4 bars set out over 3 levels. The decor is opulent with crystal chandeliers, marble columns and velvet furnishings. Funk and House.

Luxe Bar, 446 Beaufort St, Highgate, T9228 9680. Wed-Sun 2000-late. Enjoy a cocktail and the luxurious atmosphere in one of the 3 highly fashionable lounges.

Must Winebar, 519 Beaufort St, Highgate, T9328 8255, www.must.com.au. Open 1200-2400. A heaven for wine lovers that also serves superb French-style food.

Rocket Room, 174 James St (downstairs), T9328 9633. Fri-Sat 0800-0400. The place to come for live performances of rock and metal bands, including a number of album launches and local talent. It can be heavy

stuff though, so consider your ear plugs if you're heading down.

Rosie O'Grady's, corner of James and Milligan Sts, T9328 1488. Typical 'Irish' pub, dark and green cosiness and a good range of British and Irish beers. Backpacker night with drink specials Tue and Sun from 1800. Live music Wed-Sun.

Universal Wine Bar, 221 William St, T9227 6771, www.universalbar.com.au. Wed-Sun. Wed-Thu, Sun 1700-2400, Fri-Sat 1700-0200. Hip without being slick, the Universal's long room opens to the street but becomes dim and jazzy at the back. Good snack menu Wed-Sun from 1700. Live blues and jazz every night.

Subiaco and around *p31, map p31*
Subiaco Hotel, corner of Rokeby Rd and Hay St, T9381 3069. Large historic hotel refurbished in smart, contemporary style, and now the social hub of Subi. 3 main areas: edgy public bar serving up cheap counter meals, 1200-2300 with live music Thu, Sat, DJs Fri and **Subiaco Café**, the hotel's upmarket, mid-range terrace restaurant, jazz band on Wed and Sat nights. Café meals 0700-late.

Leederville *p32*
The Garden, 742 Newcastle St, T9202 8282, www.thegarden.net.au. A bar/pub attracting a slightly older crowd than the Leederville next door. Patrons can sit in the spacious beer garden and sip wine or draught beer, there is a good selection of both, and tuck in to the good quality food. There are small plates for sharing such as the cheese selection, the smoky almonds or the Fremantle octopus, or larger meals such as steak or salads. A lovely place to kick back and relax.

Hip-E Club, corner of Newcastle and Oxford Sts (rear of Leederville Village), T9227 8899, www.hipeclub.com.au. Tue-Wed and Fri from 2200, Sat from 2100. 70s, 80s and early 90s psychedelia and backpacker specials (Tue from 2000).

The Manor, Newcastle St, T9272 9893, located behind the **Hip-E Club**. French-style bar with a relaxed atmosphere in the lounge upstairs and DJ music downstairs with the 'Grand Piano' DJ desk as an eye catcher. Fri-Sat 2100-0500.

Niche, off Oxford St, T9227 1007, www.niche bar.com.au. Wed 1900-0200, Thu 2100-0200, Fri-Sat 1900-0300. Popular, fashionable bar.

Claremont *p32*

The Claremont, 1 Bay View Terr, T9286 0123, www.theclaremont.com.au. Corner pub with large terrace and lots of standing space. Inside is leather and wood, and there's a pool table. Live music or DJs Thu-Sun. Tue is quiz night, Wed there are salsa classes upstairs and on Sat all cocktails are $10.

Nedlands *p32*

Captain Stirling, 80 Stirling Highway, T9386 2200, www.captainstirlinghotel.com.au. Stylish old pub renovated in colonial style and located in the **Captain Stirling Hotel**, popular with an older crowd. Excellent food daily 1200-2200.

Cottesloe *p33*

Cottesloe is renowned for its Sun sessions. Sun afternoons in the extensive beer gardens of the '**Cott**' or the '**OBH**' attract thousands of svelte and tanned beach boys and girls. Shades, attitude and surf attire are all essential.

Cottesloe Beach Hotel, see Sleeping. The mustard-coloured art deco Cott has an ocean-facing balcony (although the view is not quite as good as the **OBH**) and a contemporary stylish bar. The Sun session is most popular here and the pub has live music from Wed-Sat. The pub also has an ATM and a pleasant colourful café, open daily for lunch, dinner Tue-Sun and breakfast on weekends.

Ocean Beach Hotel, see Sleeping. The long back bar has pool tables but the front bar is the one to head for at sunset. Picture windows overlook the ocean in a large wood-lined room.

🎭 Entertainment

The main agency is **Ticketmaster**, infoline T1900 933666, bookings T136100, www.ticketmaster.com.au. Ask for the nearest retail outlet. Theatre tickets are usually handled by **BOCS Ticketing**, T9484 1133, www.bocs ticketing.com.au. BOCS ticket outlets: Perth Concert Hall, His Majesty's Theatre, Playhouse Theatre and Subiaco Arts Centre.

Cinema

Indoor Screening details are published daily in the *West Australian* newspaper.

Ace Cinema, 500 Hay St, Subiaco, T9388 6500, www.moviemasters.com.au. Mainstream movies, parking available.

Cinema Paradiso, 164 James St, Northbridge, T9227 1771. Arthouse and mainstream features. Has a good bar and is fully licensed so patrons can enjoy a drink with their film.

Luna, 155 Oxford St, Leederville, T9444 4056, www.lunapalace.com.au. Mainstream and alternative movies. Themed double features on Mon evenings.

Windsor, 98 Stirling Highway, Nedlands, T9386 3554, www.lunapalace.com.au. Old-fashioned, small cinema, where the first subtitled film was shown in Perth. Now screens a combination of mainstream and indie flicks.

Outdoor One of the best things to do in Perth is to see a film at an outdoor cinema. You can usually take a picnic and nothing beats having a drink while you recline in a deck chair and gaze at the stars during the slow bits. Season limited to summer only (Dec-Apr).

Camelot, 16 Lochee St, Mosman Park, T9385 4793, www.lunapalace.com.au. Recent releases in a fairly classy setting, also home to the Flickerfest short film festival in Mar.

Licensed venue, bar profits support the Mosman Park Arts Foundation. Wood-fired pizzas available. No BYO.

Luna Outdoor, 155 Oxfords St, Leederville, T9444 4056, www.lunapalace.com.au. Aims to screen films that can't be seen elsewhere such as Japanese horror or cult skate flicks. Picnics OK but venue is licensed so no BYO.

Moonlight Cinema, www.moonlight. com.au. Synergy Parkland in Kings Park, screens popular favourites and cult classics (Jan-Mar). Limited number of bean beds available ($6). Tickets on the website or at the box office near the entrance from 1800.

Somerville Auditorium at UWA, T9380 1732, and **Joondalup Picture Garden**, T6304 5888, at Edith Cowan University in Joondalup both screen arthouse and foreign films from the Perth International Arts Festival (Feb-Mar). Tickets at the door or from the website www.perthfestival.com.au. Arrive by 1800 for a good seat at the picturesque Somerville.

Theatre

Contact **BOCS** for theatre tickets and current performances.

Belvoir Amphitheatre, T9296 3033, www.belvoir.net.au, and **Quarry Amphitheatre**, T9385 9263, www.quarryamphitheatre.com.au, both lovely stone amphitheatres in classical Greek style. Look out for events.

His Majesty's, 825 Hay St, T9265 0900, www.hismajestystheatre.com.au. A beautiful Edwardian theatre and the state's main venue. Also home of the WA Ballet and WA Opera companies. There is a Museum of Performing Arts here as well, Mon-Fri 1000-1600, gold coin donation entry.

Perth Concert Hall, 5 St Georges Terr, T9231 9900, www.perthconcerthall.com.au. The main venue for classical performances, particularly from the West Australian Symphony Orchestra.

Playhouse, 3 Pier St, T9323 3400, www.playhousetheatre.com.au. Modern proscenium arch theatre and home of the Perth Theatre Company, producing contemporary and classic works with local and national performers.

Regal, 474 Hay St, Subiaco, T132 849, www.regaltheatre.com.au. Puts on a wide range of local and touring shows and performers. Bookings BOCS.

Subiaco Arts Centre, 180 Hammersley Rd, Subiaco, T9380 3000, www.subiacoarts centre.com.au. A major venue set in lovely gardens near the top of Rokeby Rd. A 300-seat auditorium and smaller studio performance space. Home to the **Barking Gecko Theatre Company**, www.barkinggecko.com.au.

Yirra Yaakin Noongar Theatre, 65 Murray St, T9202 1966, www.yirra yaakin.asn.au. A Noongar company that produces Aboriginal theatre using Aboriginal writers, directors, designers and production staff.

⚙ Festivals and events

Perth has just one major festival and lacks major sporting events due to its isolation and small population. Most events are held during spring and summer.

Jan Hopman Cup, www.hopmancup. com. A tennis championship held at Burswood Dome running for a week. International teams of 1 man and woman from each country, compete against each other. Attracts some big tennis names but there are fears Perth may lose the event to another state in the next few years.

26 Jan Skyworks, held every Australia Day, is a fireworks show set to music broadcast on a local radio station. It is Perth's most popular event, attracting 400,000 people who picnic in Kings Park and along the Swan River foreshore to watch the fireworks. Get a position many hours before the show starts.

Feb Rottnest Channel Swim, www.rottnest

channelswim.com.au, about 1200 people race from Cottesloe Beach to Rottnest (20 km). It's all over pretty quickly but fun to watch the start and finish.

Feb-Mar Perth International Arts Festival, the main event of the year, including hundreds of events all over the city. This includes the best local and international theatre, opera, dance, visual arts and music. The cultural centre acts as a focus point, alive with activity from 1730-0300. A film festival is also part of the programme, held outdoors from Dec-Apr at the Somerville at UWA and Joondalup Pines at Edith Cowan University. Programs are widely available from Dec, all festival tickets from BOCS or the festival website. For more info T6488 2000, www.perthfestival.com.au.

Early Aug Avon Descent, www.avon descent.com.au, a 133-km whitewater competition on the Avon River from Northam to Perth. It's always an exciting event, involving some portage, but gets hairy when water levels are low and kayaks or rafts get stuck on rocks.

Sep Kings Park Wildflower Festival, is a huge indoor and outdoor display of native plants and flowers. This is a good way to see the state's incredible variety of wildflowers if you're not able to get to the wildflower country (mid-west region) during the Sep-Oct wildflower season. Held for about one month. Information can be found at www.bgpa.wa.gov.au.

Oct Pride Festival is a celebration of gay and lesbian arts, culture and entertainment. Ends with a fantastic parade through the streets of Northbridge and a dance party. For more info T9427 0828, www.pridewa.asn.au.

Nov-Dec Artrage Festival, T9227 6288, www.artrage.com.au. Alternative arts festival including theatre, dance, music, street performers, comedy and visual arts. Perth and Fremantle.

🛒 Shopping

Shopping hours are Mon-Thu 0830-1730 with late-night shopping until 2100 in the city and Fremantle on Fri, and in the suburbs on Thu. Sat hours are 0830-1700. On Sun, city hours are 1100-1700, Fremantle 1000-1800.

Central Perth *p24, map p26*
Perth's compact shopping area consists of the parallel Hay St and Murray St Malls and the arcades connecting them. The shopping also continues west along Hay St as far as King St, which is a trendy pocket of high-end fashion and homewares shopping, galleries and cafes. The city has 2 major department stores, **Myers** in Forrest Pl, and **David Jones** occupying a block between the Malls. These both sell almost everything and David Jones has an excellent food hall.

Arts and crafts
Aspects of Kings Park, Fraser Av, Kings Park, T9480 3900, www.aspectsofkings park.com.au, daily 0900-1700. Top quality gallery and gift shop, owned by the Botanic Gardens and Parks Authority and featuring works by local artists that reflect on the natural environment. There is also a good selection of natural history titles.

Creative Native, 58 Forrest Chase, Forrest Pl, T9221 5800, www.creativenative.com.au. Open 0900-1700. Large commercial Aboriginal art gallery and shop. Also good books on Aboriginal art.

Form Contemporary Art and Design, 357 Murray St, T9226 2799, www.form.net.au. Mon-Thu 0900-1730, Fri 0900-1800, Sat 0900-1700. A shop featuring the very best of contemporary Australian design, including ceramics, glass work, jewellery, textiles, sculpture and woodwork.

Books and maps
The main chains are **Dymocks**, **Borders**, both in Hay St Mall, and **Angus and Robertson**, in

the Murray St Mall, diagonally across from the entrance to Myers. These chains can also be found in suburban shopping centres.

All Foreign Language Bookshop, 572 Hay St, T9485 1246. Mon-Sat 0930-1700, Fri 0930-1900, Sat 1030-1600. Dictionaries, some foreign language titles and language learning tools such as tapes and books. The usual French and Spanish, but also Laotian, Swahili and books on Macedonian poetry.

Boffins, 806 Hay St, T9321 5755, www.boffinsbookshop.com.au. Mon-Thu 0900-1730, Fri 0900-2000, Sat 0900-1700, Sun 1200-1700. An independent selling practical, technical and special interest books. It has a travel section on the ground floor.

Elizabeth's Second-hand Bookshop, 820 Hay St, T9481 8848. Perth's best second-hand range. Also suburban branches including 375 Roberts Rd, Subiaco, T9381 5886 and a number in Fremantle.

Fantasy Planet, 8 Shafto Lane, T9481 8393. Sci-fi and fantasy. Mon-Thu 1000-1800, Fri 1000-2100, Sat 0930-1730.

The Perth Map Centre, 900 Hay St, T9322 5733, www.mapworld.com.au. Mon-Fri 0900-1730, Sat 1000-1500. Maps and guidebooks for every state and country. Full range of topographic maps, also Munda Biddi maps, Bibbulmun and Cape-to-Cape track maps. See also **Art Gallery of WA** (page 24), **WA Museum** (page 25) and **Alexander Library** (page 25).

Clothes

Outback Red, Plaza Arcade. Bushwear such as boots, hats and moleskins.

R M Williams, upstairs in the Carillion Arcade. Sell rugged countrywear such as boots, hats and moleskins.

Surf & Skate, 328 Murray St. Good surfwear and wide range of flip flops.

Underground Surf Sports, corner Plaza Arcade and Hay St Mall. Good for surf and swimwear.

Wheels & Dollbaby, 26 King St, T9481 8488,

www.wheelsanddollbaby.com.au. Mon-Thu and Sat 1000-1800, Fri 1000-2100, Sun 1100-1700. Vintage and rockabilly inspired fashion, popular with celebrities and with a price tag to match.

Jewellery

The city centre is awash with jewellery shops. For cheaper imported jewellery try the Fremantle markets.

Antika, Shop 39 London Court, T9325 3352. There's nowhere better for silver jewellery.

Rosendorff's, 673 Hay St Mall, T9321 4015, www.rosendorffs.com. One of the best, for Argyle diamonds, Broome pearls and Australian opal in a classy environment.

Markets

The king of Perth markets is actually to be found in Fremantle. These markets are fairly permanent, well-established affairs.

Canning Vale Markets, 280 Bannister Rd, Canning Vale, T9455 1389, www.canningvale markets.com, just east of Jandakot airport. Huge flea market with hundreds of stalls. Sun 0700-1530. During the week this is WA's biggest undercover wholesale market for meat, fish, flowers and fruit and veg. Clearance sale on Sat.

Wanneroo Market, 33 Prindiville Dr, Wanneroo, 22 km north of city centre, T9409 8397. Fri, Sat and Sun 0900-1700. A huge a/c indoor market selling everything and anything. Also has a food court.

Music

78 Records, 914 Hay St, T9322 6384, www.78records.com.au. Mon-Thu 0900-1730, Fri 0900-1900, Sat 0900-1700, Sun 1200-1700. Huge selection, also ticket outlet for gigs and sells music mags.

Beat Route, 37 Barrack St, T9218 9981, www.beatrouterecords.com.au. New and second-hand vinyl, as well as CDs and books.

Wesley Classics, 800 Hay St, opposite Wesley Arcade, T9321 1978,

www.wesleyclassics. com.au. Mon-Fri
0900-1730, Sat 0900-1700. Classical CDs.

Outdoor

The outdoor shops are all clustered together
on Hay Street, a number sell maps for the
Bibbulmun and Cape-to-Cape tracks,
as well as the Munda Biddi Trail.

Kathmandu, 895 Hay St,
www.kathmandu.com.au.

Mainpeak, 858 Hay St, T9322 9044,
www.mainpeak.com.au. Mon-Thu 0900-1800,
Fri 0900-2100, Sat 0900-1700, Sun 1200-1700.
Well-stocked store, strong on local knowledge.
Trekking slide shows year-round, also hire of
almost all gear except boots. There are 2 other
stores at 31 and 35 Jarrad St, Cottesloe, T9385
2552, which also hire out sea kayaks.

Mountain Designs, 862 Hay St, T9322 4774,
www.mountaindesigns.com.

Paddy Pallin, 884 Hay St, T9321 2666,
www.paddypallin.com.au.

Northbridge and around *p29, map p30*

There are number of interesting small
boutiques in Northbridge, and most can
be found on William St. The many Asian
supermarkets are on William St between
Newcastle and Brisbane.

Fi & Co, 289 William St, T9328 6007,
www.fiandco.com. Beautiful new and vintage
clothes (for men and women), as well as
colourful shoes and accessories.

Kakulas Brothers, 183 William St, T9328
5744, www.kakulasbros.com.au. Fantastic
shop, with towers of spices and self-serve vats
of pulses, nuts and dried fruit. Also offers
delicatessen food such as cheese and meats.
Stocks imported goods; English jam and
squash, Swiss chocolate and Greek tea.
Reasonably priced and offers takeaway,
freshly ground coffee.

Subiaco and around *p31, map p31*

Rokeby Rd is a good spot for clothes shopping.

Chokeby Rd, 175 Rokeby Rd, Subiaco, T9481

1144. Chocolate specialists, bursting with
both hand-crafted and European goodies.

Earth Market, 14/375 Subiaco Mews, Hay St,
Subiaco, T9382 2266, www.earthmarket.
com.au. Mon-Fri 0900-1800, Sat 0900-1700.
Organic food store and café.

Kailis Fish Market, 101 Oxford St,
Leederville, T9443 6300,
www.kailisbrosleederville. com.au. Daily
0700-1800. Every kind of fresh fish and
seafood available relatively close to the city
centre.

Linney's, 37 Rokeby Rd, Subiaco. Mon,
Wed, Fri 0930-1700, Tue 1000-1700, Thu
0930-2000, Sat 0930-1600. Specializes
in WA pearls, diamonds and gold.

Mr Sparrow, 223 Bagot Rd, Subiaco, T9381
6362, www.mrsparrow.com.au. Mon-Fri
0930-1730, Sat 1000-1700. A boutique selling
interesting jewellery, homewares and
gardening gifts.

Oxford St Books, 119 Oxford St, Leederville,
T9443 9844. Open until 2230 every night.
A good range of books and helpful staff.

Rockeby Records, 16A Rokeby Rd, Subiaco,
T9381 5126. Has a big mainstream range.

Subiaco Bookshop, 113 Rockeby Rd, T9382
1945. An independent with a interesting
selection of titles. The tables are bound to
yield some treasures.

Tea for Me, corner of Rokeby Rd and Church
St, Subacio, T9380 9377, www.teaforme.
com.au. Mon-Fri 0930-1700, Sat until 1600.
Nearly 100 different flavoured Ceylon teas,
available in leaf or as teabags. Also sells
exquisite ceramic tea sets.

Nedlands and Claremont *p32*

The best clothes shopping is found in
Subiaco and Claremont. Bay View and St
Quentins Terraces in Claremont are full of
fashion boutiques, and it is shoe heaven
with a number of good shoe shops.

Claremont Fresh, 333 Stirling Highway,
Claremont, T9383 3066. Daily 0700-1900.
A fruit and veg market, also selling seafood,

bread and some groceries.

Fresh Provisions, 303 Stirling Highway, **Bayview Shopping Centre**, Claremont, T9383 3308, www.provisions.com.au. A small supermarket open 0900-2200.

The Lane Bookshop, 52C Old Theatre Lane, Claremont, T9384 4423, www.lanebook. com.au. Mon-Wed and Fri 0900-1730, Thu 0900-2100, Sat 0900-1700, Sun 1030-1330. Fine range of literary, arts and travel titles and knowledgeable, helpful staff.

Peter's Choice Butchery, 3 St Quentin Av, Claremont, T9383 3637. Sells takeaway pastas and curries by weight.

Zenith Music, 309 Stirling Highway, **Bayview Shopping Centre**, Claremont, T9383 1422, www.zenithmusic.com. One of Perth's most comprehensive selections of CDs, also instruments and sheet music.

Zomp, 2 Bayview Terr, Claremont, T9384 6250, www.zomp.com.au. A wide range of good-quality women's shoes, from sky-high heels to biker boots. There's another branch on King St in Perth CBD.

South Perth *p32*

Mill Point Caffé Bookshop 254 Mill Point Rd, South Perth, T9367 4567. Daily 0830-1730. Knowledgeable staff and a pleasant café.

▲▲ Activities and tours

AFL (Australian rules)

West Coast Eagles and the *Fremantle Dockers* both play at the Subiaco Oval. Each have home games, once a fortnight on either a Sat or Sun, from the end of Mar to Aug. See www.afl.com.au for fixtures. Tickets from **Ticketmaster**, T1300 136100. Tickets go on sale 2 weeks before a match and often sell out, so it's best to book.

Backpacker buses

Easyrider, T1300 308477, www.easyrider tours.com.au. Offers hop-on hop-off transport up to Exmouth, Broome and the southwest.

Nullarbor Traveller, T8687 0457 and T1800 816858, www.the-traveller.com.au. Runs excellent 9-day adventure trips to Adelaide ($1350, concessions $1295) that include swimming with tuna, departing most Sun at 0700 from Welling St coach rank. There is also a 6-day camping trip from Perth to Esperance ($770, concessions $740).

Boat cruises

For maximum time at Rottnest, take an early trip from Fremantle. Several companies operate cruises on the Swan River from the Barrack St Jetty.

Captain Cook Cruises, Pier 3, Barrack St, T9325 3341, www.captaincookcruises. com.au. Cruises range from short runs to Fremantle, lunch and dinner cruises (around $64-99), to gourmet wine-tasting trips upriver to Swan Valley ($146).

Mills Charters, T9246 5334, www.mills charters.com.au. Heads out from Hillarys Boat Harbour (see page 35) for deep-sea fishing most days of the week (depending on demand) at 0630 ($185 weekdays, $210 weekends). Also offers 3-hr whale-watching trips ($80, concessions $65, children $55) departing Tue, Thu, Sat and Sun at 0900. Night-fishing trips run Fri and Sat 1730-0200.

Rottnest Express, Pier 2, Barrack St Jetty, T1300 467688, www.rottnestexpress.com.au. Day returns to Rottnest for $79.50, Also offers accommodation packages, and bike and snorkel gear hire.

Rottnest Fast Ferries, Hillarys Boat Harbour (see page 35), T9246 1039, www.rottnest fastferries.com.au. Day returns to Rottnest for $82. Offers accommodation packages, bike hire, snorkel hire and also options that combine a cruise around Rottnest with surf lessons or entry to the aquarium. Whale-watching tours run Sep-Dec (2 hrs) and cost $62, children $36, concessions $51. Pick-ups available from Perth.

Cricket
WACA, T9265 7222, www.waca.com.au.
The state side *Western Warriors* play during
summer. The ground also occasionally hosts
international matches.

Cycling tours
Remote Outback Cycle Tours, T03445
4927, T1800 157830, www.cycletours.com.au.
Offers superb 4WD and cycle combination
tours, including from Perth to Uluru, $4420,
24 days.

Diving
Aqwa, Hillarys Boat Harbour (see page 35),
T9447 7500. You can arrange to scuba dive or
snorkel with the sharks. Daily 1300 and 1500,
$175-199.
Australian Diving Academy, T9356 9677,
www.ausdiving.com.au. Runs PADI courses
and dive trips to Rottnest.

Golf
Perth has excellent courses that welcome
visitors and have relatively low fees.
Burswood Park, Roger Mackay Dr,
Burswood, T9470 2992,
www.burswoodparkgolfcourse. com. Great
city views. Equipment hire.
Vines Resort, Verdelho Dr, Swan Valley,
T9297 3000, www.vines.com.au. A 36-hole
championship course along banks of Ellen
Brook, good facilities nearby at the resort.
Wembley, The Boulevard, Floreat, T9484
2500, www.wembleygolf.com.au. Two
18-hole layouts, also driving range,
pro shop and bar.

Kayaking and rafting
Rivergods, 3/10 Whyalla St, Willetton, T9259
0749, www.rivergods.com.au. Heads out daily
Sep-Jun to Penguin Island off Rockingham
to see the penguins and seals ($139,
concessions $125, children $95). Trips
further afield and personalized
canoeing/rafting trips available.

Kitesurfing
This fast-growing sport of surfing harnessed
to a parachute offers awesome power and
speed, and is generally practised off the
beaches between Cottesloe and Fremantle.
Choice Kitesurfing, 4/54 Rockingham Rd,
Hamilton Hill, T9336 7884, www.choice
kitesurfing.com.au. Lessons, beginners
$160 for 2 hrs. Unlimited free lessons if
purchasing a kite and board package.

Parasailing
South Perth Parasailing, Mill Point Rd,
T0408 382 595, www.southperthpara
sailing.com.au. Daily in summer (weather
permitting). Single $80, tandem $140.

Sailing
Funcats, Coode St Jetty, South Perth,
T0408 926003, www.funcats.com.au.
Daily 0930-1830, Oct-Apr. Surfcat hire
for $30 per hr, free tuition (1-3 people).
Wind Dancer, Hillarys Boat Harbour,
T9448 2496. Available for charter for a
wide range of sailing excursions ($650 per
day, max 12 passengers) and also heads
out for half-day cruises about once a week
depending on demand ($35 per person).

Scenic flights
Rottnest Air Taxi, T9292 5027 and T1800
500006, www.rottnest.de. Offers a range of
flights from Jandakot Airport. A 35-min flight
over Perth, and Rottnest is $100, minimum
2 people.

Skydiving
WA Skydiving Academy, 48 William St,
Northbridge, T9227 6066 and T1300 137855,
www.waskydiving.com.au. Accelerated
freefall $550. Perth City tandem jumps
Mon-Thu $450-530. Pinjarra tandem
jumps $240-400.

Surfing and bodyboarding
There is an artificial reef called Cables, south of

Cottesloe Beach, ensuring consistent breaks all year round. **Whalebone Classic** is a Malibu competition attracting about 5000 people over a weekend in mid-Jul.

Fun's Back Surf, 120 Marine Parade, T9284 7873. A good point of ontact for information. Surfboard hire is $35, snorkel gear $25.

Vision Surf, Esplanade, T9245 3227. Hires out surfboards for $30/2 hrs, bodyboards for $25 for 2 hrs and wetsuits for $10 a day.

Tour operators

Out & About, T9377 3376, www.outandabouttourscom.au. Takes small groups to visit wineries plus the chocolate and cheese factories. All tours include lunch/dinner, free pick-up and drop-off in Perth. Prices between $95-135.

Planet Perth, T9225 6622, www.planet tours.com.au. Tours to the Pinnacles, Monkey Mia and the Southwest.

Swan Valley Tours, T9274 1199, www.svtours.com.au. Swan Valley tours, wine tasting, cheese tastings, a visit to a microbrewery, the nougat factory, the chocolate factory and Guildford. Also offers cruise options. $65-130 including lunch.

Two Feet and a Heartbeat, www.twofeet.com.au. Evening walking tours of Perth. The main tour is one of the CBD where the guide tells stories and provides information on the history and architecture, 2 hrs, $40 (only $20 on Tue). The tour starts at 1730 and ends with a drink in **Rosie O'Grady's** in Northbridge. Another option is a tour of Perth's small bars (3 hrs) for $40, including tapas and drinks tasting. Shopping tours run on the last Sat of the month ($89) and include lunch and a chat with a stylist.

Urban Aboriginal Tours, T0403 529473, www.urbanindigenoustours.com. An opportunity to indulge in contemporary Aboriginal Australia by visiting suburban art studios, meeting with local Aboriginal artists, sampling contemporary bush foods and stopping for lunch at a local Indigenous café.

The day ends with a didgeridoo workshop. $125, concessions $110.

Western Xposure, T9371 3695 and T1800 621200, www.westernxposure.com.au. For direct 4WD trips to Alice Springs. It also heads down to the southwest and up around the coast as far as Darwin.

Waterskiing

Extreme Ski WA, Narrows Bridge, South Perth, T0417 792118, www.extremeskiwa. com. Oct-Apr Tue-Sun, May-Sep Sun. Water-skiing and wakeboarding is $35 for 15 mins (free coaching), tubing $20 for 15 mins.

⊖ Transport

Air

Skywest flies daily to **Albany**, **Broome**, **Carnarvon** (Tue, Thu, Fri, Sat and Sun), **Esperance** (Sun-Fri), **Exmouth** (Sun-Fri), **Geraldton**, **Kalgoorlie** (Sun-Fri), and **Port Hedland** (Wed-Sat). **Qantas** provides daily flights to **Broome**, **Kalgoorlie**, **Karratha** and **Port Hedland**. It also has daily flights to most state capitals (except Hobart) and **Alice Springs**. **Virgin Blue** flies daily to **Adelaide**, **Broome**, **Melbourne** and **Sydney**.

Airlines Air New Zealand, 178 St George's Terr, T9442 6077. **British Airways**, 77 St Georges Terr, T9425 5333. **Garuda Indonesia**, 40 The Esplanade, T9321 5100. **Malaysia Airlines**, 56 William St, T9263 7007. **Qantas**, 55 William St, T131313. **Royal Brunei**, 216 St George's Terr, T9321 8757 or 131223. **Singapore Airlines**, 178 St George's Terr, T9479 8166 or 131011 **Skywest**, Perth Domestic Airport, T9477 8301 or 1300 660088. **South African Airways**, Perth International Airport, T9477 1314. **Virgin Blue**, T136789.

Bicycle

Perth is ideal for cycling and there a number of bike shops that will hire out gear for good prices. Pick up detailed maps of cycle routes: *Bikewest Perth Bike Map Series* is good.

About Bike Hire, Causeway car park, corner Plain St and Riverside Drive, East Perth, T9221 2665, www.aboutbikehire.com.au. Apr-Nov daily 0900-1700 and Dec-Mar 0900-1800. $36 for 24-hr rental. Prices drop if hiring for more than 1 day.

Cycle Centre, 282 Hay St, opposite Perth Mint, T9325 1176. Mon-Fri 0900-1730, Sat 0900-1500, Sun 1300-1600. Hires bikes for $25 a day.

Bus

Local The free city centre buses, CATs, T136213 take 3 circuits. **Blue Cat** travels around Northbridge, through city centre, and around Riverside Drive and Mounts Bay Rd. Buses every 7 mins Mon-Fri 0650-1820, and every 15 mins on Fri 1820-0100, Sat 0830-0100, and Sun 1000-1700. **Red Cat** heads to East Perth just short of the WACA, and to West Perth as far as Outram St. The service runs much of the length of Hay St in a westerly direction, and Murray St the other way. Buses every 5 mins Mon-Fri 0650-1820, and every 25 mins Sat-Sun 1000-1815. The **Yellow Cat** operates in a loop from East Perth to West Perth, from Claisebrook train station along Wellington St to the Princess Margaret Hospital. Buses every 10 mins Mon-Fri 0650-1820, and every 30 mins Sat-Sun 1000-1815. All 3 services run within 200 m of the Wellington St Station, the Blue Cat stops at both the Esplanade Busport and Barrack Sq (for the Barrack St Jetty). No CAT services on public holidays.

Selected bus services from Wellington St Bus Station: **Airport** (domestic terminal), 37; **Fremantle** (Queen St and/or Railway Station) via **East Perth**, 103, 106, 160; **Kalamunda**, 283, 296, 299; **Kings Park Rd**, **Nedlands**, **Claremont**, 102, 103.

Long distance The majority of services are run by the state-owned company **TransWA**, Perth Business Centre and main stations, T1300 662205, www.transwa.wa.gov.au, whose routes extend right around the southwest, east as far as Norseman, and north as far as Kalbarri and Meekatharra. There are a handful of other operators that may prove more convenient. **South West Coachlines**, 3 Mounts Bay Rd, T9324 2333, www.southwestcoachlines.com.au, has a couple of southern routes, including one terminating at **Dunsborough**, and another to **Manjimup**. Integrity, 554 Wellington St, T1800 226339 and T9226 1339, www.integritycoachlines.com.au, runs a route up the **Great Northern Highway** via **Meekatharra** and **Newman** to **Port Hedland** (departing Perth Wed 0900, arriving in Port Hedland Thu 1900). Given the sparsity of land transport in some parts of the state, **Greyhound**, East Perth Terminal, T1300 473946, www.greyhound.com.au, usually considered an interstate operator only, provides a few further, very useful options. Their main northbound service leaves Perth (East Perth bus station) at 0730, travels up the Great Northern Highway through **Geraldton**, stops at **Port Hedland** on the way up to **Broome**. This continues on via **Kununurra** and **Katherine** to **Darwin** (60 hrs). **Selected services** TransWA routes from Perth Railway Station or East Perth Terminal: **Albany** via **Mount Barker**, daily, GS1, GS2; **Albany** via **Timber towns**, daily, GS3; **Bunbury**, **Cape-to-Cape** towns, Sun-Fri, SW1; **Geraldton** via **Dongara**, Sun-Fri, N1; **Geraldton** via **Kalbarri**, Sun-Fri, N1; **Northam**, **York**, Sun-Wed, Fri, GS2; **Pemberton** via **Cape-to-Cape towns**, Sun-Thu, SW1; **Pemberton** via **Bunbury**, Mon, Wed, Sun, SW2.

Car

Perth is a fairly easy place to get around by car and there are no special restrictions or toll fees. The freeways are the arterial routes and entry and exit points are marked by large green signs. Kwinana Freeway services the southern suburbs, the Mitchell Freeway services the northern suburbs. The Graham Farmer Freeway is a short stretch just north

Ticket to ride

Transperth routes extend beyond Hillarys to the north, out to the Swan Valley and Perth Hills, and south as far as Mandurah. Fares are worked out according to how many zones you cross. The central suburbs are encompassed by zone 1, and zone 2 extends to include Fremantle, Cottesloe, Scarborough and Midland. Tickets are valid for two to three hours, and cost $2.50 for travel within one zone, $3.70 for two zones. A multi-zone *DayRider* ticket is available for $9 after 0900 and is valid all day. *FamilyRider* ticket is a real bargain: two adults, plus up to five children, travel anywhere and back for $9. It's available all day weekends, after 0900 school holiday weekdays, after 1800 Monday-Thursday, and 1500 Friday. Standard tickets, *DayRiders* and *FamilyRiders* can be purchased on board buses and ferries, and at train stations. If travellers are going to be in Perth for a month or more it is worth investing in a *SmartRider*, an electronic ticket to which value is added. Don't forget to tag on and tag off if using it. For more information take a look at www.transperth.wa.gov.au or call the infoline on T136213.

of the city centre that connects the Mitchell Freeway to the Great Eastern Highway (and airports). The speed limit in built-up areas is 50 kph, unless signposted otherwise.
Car hire **Bayswater**, 160 Adelaide Terr, T9325 1000, www.bayswatercarrental.com.au, is one of the best value of many operators in the city, though they do not have a depot at either airport terminal.
Car parking Council car parks in Roe St, behind train station. Restricted meters in the city centre, several car parks off Riverside Drive and better value ones by the WACA. For more information on car park, see www.perth.wa.gov.au/parking.
Car servicing **Ultra Tune**, 25 Newcastle St, Northbridge, T9227 5356, www.ultratune.com.au, has many other branches in the city.

Ferry
See also Boat cruises, above.
Transperth operates ferries from Barrack Street Jetty over to South Perth. Those to Mends St are the best for the zoo and main restaurants and leave every 20-30 mins daily from 0750-1924, and also to 2115 on Fri-Sat in Sep-Apr. Last return ferry is at 1930 (2130 Fri-Sat during Sep-Apr).

Taxi
There are dozens of taxi ranks around the city. A few are: outside Perth Station on Wellington St, southwest corner of junction of Adelaide Terr and Hill St, opposite the Melbourne on south side of Hay St. Also **Black & White**, T131008, www.blackandwhitetaxis.com.au. **Swan**, T131330, www.swantaxis.com.au.

Train
Local There are 5 suburban lines radiating like spokes from Perth station. All run regular services from early morning to past midnight. To the north the Joondalup line stops at **Leederville** and **Stirling** (change for Scarborough Beach) on the way, while the Fremantle line calls at **Subiaco**, **Claremont** and **Cottesloe** (with a 15-min walk to the beach). The Midland line has stops at **East Perth** (for TransWA services) and **Guildford** (the Swan Valley), and trains to **Armadale** call at **Burswood**. The Mandurah line runs via **Murdoch**, **Cockburn** and **Rockingham**. Fares are as per the bus services.
Long distance TransWA, Perth Business Centre and main stations, T1300 662205 or T9326 2600, www.transwa.wa.gov.au, most useful rail services are the *Prospector* line to

Toodyay, **Northam** and **Kalgoorlie**, the *Australind* line to **Bunbury** and the *AvonLink* to **Avon Valley**. *The Indian Pacific*, T132147, www.gsr.com.au, heads to **Adelaide** (43 hrs) and **Sydney** (70 hrs) at 1155 on Wed and Sun.

Directory

Banks The major banks have ATMs on Hay St Mall and Murray St Mall. They are also liberally located in all the central suburbs. Foreign exchange: **American Express**, 645 Hay St, T9221 0693. Mon-Fri 0900-1700, Sat 0900- 1200. **Embassies and consulates** Canada, 267 St George's Terr, T9322 7930. Germany, 8th floor, St George's Court, 16 St George's Terr, T9325 8851. **Irish Republic**, 10 Lilika Rd, City Beach, T9385 8247. **Italy**, 1292 Hay St, T9322 4500. **Japan**, Level 21, The Forrest Centre, 221 St George's Terr, T9480 1800. **Netherlands**, 1/88 Thomas St, T9486 1579. **Spain**, 23 Barrack St, T9225 5222. **Sweden**, Courier Australia, 23 Walters Dr, Herdsman, T9204 0900. **UK**, Level 26, Allendale Sq, 77 St George's Terr, T9224 4700. **USA**, 13th floor, St George's Court, 16 St George's Terr, Perth, T9202 1224.

Internet Free at Alexander Library, 1 hr only, booking required, T9427 3104, or 20 mins on the express terminals. Free Wi-Fi available at the **Perth Cultural Centre** and in Northbridge Piazza. **Medical services** 24-hr chemists: Beaufort Street Chemist, 647 Beaufort St, Mt Lawley, T9328 7775. Dentists: Lifecare Dental, 419 Wellington St, T9221 2777. Daily 0800- 2000. **Medicare**, T132011. For claims or to register visit city office 81 St George's Terr. **Hospitals: Royal Perth**, Wellington St, City, T9224 2244. **Sir Charles Gairdner**, Hospital Av, Nedlands, T9346 3333. **Medical centres: Perth Medical Centre**, 713 Hay St, T9481 4342, bulk bills. Mon-Thu 0800-1800, Fri 0800-1700, Sat 1000-1400. **Police** 1 Hay St, East Perth, T9222 1432. **Post** Forrest Pl, Mon-Fri 0830-1730, Sat 0900-1230. **Poste Restante** (take photo ID) 66 St George's Terr, Mon-Fri 0800-1700.

Contents

Footprint features

Around Perth

Fremantle

Ports are not usually known for their charm but Fremantle is a fine exception. Founded at the same time as Perth, Fremantle has kept the 19th-century buildings that Perth has lost and retained its character and spirit. A strong community of immigrants and artists contribute to the port city's alternative soul. Freo, as the locals call it, is full of street performers, markets, galleries, pubs and restaurants as well as fishing boats and container ships. Many Southern Europeans have settled here and their simple Italian cafés have merged into the busy cappuccino strip of the olive-tree-lined South Terrace. Fishing Boat Harbour has become an alternative hub of eating and entertainment activity, and manages to mix some seriously good restaurants in with some of the country's biggest fish and chip shops. Fremantle's lively atmosphere draws people from all over Perth, particularly at weekends, and it makes an interesting base for travellers.

Ins and outs → *20 km from Perth centre, 7 km from Cottesloe. For listings, see pages 65-71.*

Getting there

The private **Fremantle Airport Shuttle** ① *T9457 7150, www.fremantleairportshuttle. com.au*, runs between Perth airport and Fremantle and offers a door-to-door service from terminal to hotel if booked in advance. Fares are $30 single, $40 for two, add $10 for each additional passenger for groups of up to four. They will soon be running a timetable service and this will cost $15 per person. A cheaper ($3.70, concessions $1.50) but much longer option from the domestic terminal is to take the No 37 bus to the Esplanade Busport (see page 25) and change. A taxi will cost around $55. The main service between the Esplanade Busport and Fremantle is the 106, which runs every 30 minutes daily 0845-2100, then 2115, 2215 and 2315; the journey takes about 45 minutes (single tickets $3.70, concessions $1.50). The train runs from Perth to Fremantle regularly throughout the day and the journey takes about half an hour ($3.70, concessions $1.50). ▶▶ *See Transport, page 70.*

Getting around

Fremantle is a good city to wander around on foot, however if you want to try something a bit different hire a scooter (see page 70). Alternatively, the free Fremantle CAT circles around the town in a figure of eight that stretches from the railway station to the Arts Centre, and from Victoria Quay to south of the hospital. Buses leave every 10 minutes or so Monday-Friday 0730-1830 and Saturday-Sunday 1000-1830.

Tourist information

The Travel Lounge ① *16 Market St, T9335 1614, www.thetravellounge.com.au, Mon-Fri 0800- 2000, Sat-Sun 1000-1800,* acts as a general booking agent and net café and is also happy to provide information and advice to all travellers. The **VIC** ① *Kings Sq, T9431 7878, www.fremantle.com.au, Mon-Fri 0900-1700, Sat 1000-1500, Sun 1130-1430,* is located in the town hall and is also runs a tours and accommodation booking service. Also try www.visitfremantle.com.au.

Sights

There are some interesting historic sights in Freo but it is also well worth having a walk around the well-preserved port precinct of the west end. Phillimore Street and Cliff Street, and the surrounding streets, contain some lovely Victorian buildings, such as the Customs House. If exploring Freo's sights on foot, there are plenty of refuelling café-stops.

The Round House

① *Between High St and Bathers Bay, T9336 6897, 1030-1530, gold coin donation, volunteer guides available if visitors want to know more.*

As convicts did not reach the Swan River colony until 1850, Western Australia's oldest building need not necessarily be a gaol, but the fact remains that it is. Not actually round, the 12-sided 1831 building was built on the commanding promontory of Arthur Head, and the precinct still affords good views over the boat harbour and across to offshore islands. Built as a prison for immigrant and native wrong-doers, it was too small to house the large number of British convicts and slowly became redundant, last being used as a lock-up in 1900. For a while it was used as police living quarters, but fell into disuse when the headland became a favoured site for defensive gun batteries. The precinct has also been the site of lighthouses and, from 1900-1937, a Time Ball, looked to by mariners and locals alike to accurately fix their timepieces. A mock-up of the apparatus has been erected and is activated, complete with the accompanying cannon-fire, every day at 1300.

Port Authority Building

① *1 Cliff St, T9430 3555, www.fremantleports.com.au.*

Fremantle's docks are just north of the Roundhouse and from Victoria Quay you can often see massive ships loaded with sheep for live export negotiating the narrow passage. Presiding over all shipping movements is the modern Port Authority; its tower is far higher than any other structure in Freo.

Western Australian Maritime Museum

① *Victoria Quay Rd, T9431 8444, www.museum.wa.gov.au/maritime, main museum Thu-Tue 0930-1700, $10, children $3, concessions $5; submarine tours Thu-Tue every 30 mins, 1000-1600 (1 hr), $8, children $3, concessions $5 (buy ticket at museum first, joint tickets available for $15, children $5, concessions $8); Shipwreck Galleries, Cliff St, 0930-1700, gold coin donation.*

The striking Western Australian Maritime Museum sits on the quay looking out towards the western horizon. The six themed galleries look at WA's past and future as a community on the edge of the Indian Ocean. With significant historic objects and boats that highlight the state's sporting and adventure heritage (such as *Australia II*, the yacht that wrestled the America's cup from the USA in 1983), the exhibitions tell many fascinating stories of human endeavour. Part of the new museum, the *Oberon* class submarine **HMAS Ovens**, was commissioned in 1969 and saw active service for over 25

Fremantle

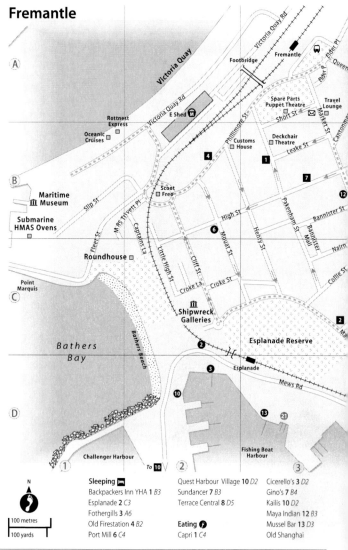

N

100 metres
100 yards

years. It is 90 m long and had a crew of over 60. Today it is in dry-dock and part of the WA Maritime Museum. The submarine is in very much the state it was when decommissioned in 1995, giving a rare glimpse into the strange lives of the submariners who crewed it. The fascinating and entertaining tours are conducted by volunteers, many of whom are

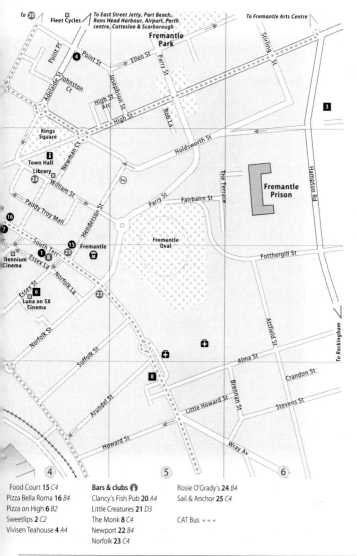

Food Court **15** C4
Pizza Bella Roma **16** B4
Pizza on High **6** B2
Sweetlips **2** C2
Vivisen Teahouse **4** A4

Bars & clubs
Clancy's Fish Pub **20** A4
Little Creatures **21** D3
The Monk **8** C4
Newport **22** B4
Norfolk **23** C4

Rosie O'Grady's **24** B4
Sail & Anchor **25** C4

CAT Bus = = =

former or serving submariners.

Housed in a complex of old dock buildings the original Maritime Museum is now called the **Shipwreck Galleries** and is primarily dedicated to the preservation and display of artefacts from the principal WA shipwrecks, mostly of the Dutch East India Company. Intermingled with the recoveries are numerous charts, logs and journals from the period and the combination presents an interesting historical overview of European exploration of Australia's west coast. There is everything from cannon to candelabra recovered from wrecks such as the *Zuytdorp* and the *Zeewijk*, but the most fascinating gallery has to be the one dedicated to the *Batavia*. A large part of the ship's hull is on display, plus a replica cabin, and most chillingly of all the hacked skeleton of one of those murdered on the Abrolhos Islands (see box, page).

Fremantle Prison

① *1 The Terrace, T9336 9200, www.fremantleprison.com.au. Entry by tour only, every 30 mins 1000-1700 (1 hr), $18, children $9.50, concessions $15 (choose between Doing Time Tour and Great Escapes Tour or do both for $24, children $15.50, concessions $21). Torchlight tours Wed and Fri evening, bookings required, $24, children $14, concessions $20. Tunnels tours run regularly from 0900, bookings required, $59, children $39, concessions $49.*

With the first consignment of convicts in 1850 it became clear to the governors of the Swan River colony that a much bigger prison than the Roundhouse would be required. The building of Fremantle Prison was one of the first tasks to be undertaken by the first convict groups and took about five years to construct. In this time they built themselves a prodigious set of buildings in a huge walled enclosure, the main cell block dominating and brooding over an expansive parade ground. Such was the solidity of construction that the prison was still in use as recently as 1991.

Fremantle Arts Centre

① *1 Finnerty St, T9432 9555, www.fac.org.au, 1000-1700, free.*

Set on a low hill overlooking the main town is an impressive but imposing Gothic limestone building dating back to the 1860s. It was built by the convicts to house those of their colleagues who had gone mad and were deemed a danger to fellow inmates and their jailers, but although still a part of the convict system it seems to have been built with considerably more flair than the stolid penitentiary just down the road. It remained an asylum, for both convicts and immigrants, until 1909 when the last of the patients were transferred to new premises in Claremont. It was planned to be allowed to run down, but at the last moment was deemed suitable as a shelter for elderly women. The US Navy took it over as their HQ during the Second World War, after which the buildings existence hung in the balance, sometimes in the shadow of imminent demolition, always gradually deteriorating. The building was finally converted to a museum and arts centre between 1965 and 1972, the museum closed in 2009. The magnificent wooden staircases and floors and spacious high-ceilinged rooms are ideal for its current purpose as an arts centre. The centre is run by a dynamic arts organization and is well worth a visit. It holds regular exhibitions of contemporary visual arts and crafts, runs arts courses and literary events, acts as a small but respected publisher and hosts free music in the courtyard every Sunday 1400-1600 (January-April). The music ranges from jazz and folk to funk and classical and, played under several large shady trees, is an excellent escape from the summer heat. Pick up a program of events at the VIC or at the centre itself. There is also a great craft shop selling the best of local work at good prices and a small bookshop. The leafy courtyard café serves cakes, coffee and light, healthy lunches (daily 1000-1600; shorter hours in winter).

Beaches
There's a beach just to the north of the harbour, but it's not the area's best. Head north of the river to **Port** and **Leighton** beaches or head south. Port Beach is a safe swimming beach, although like all west coast beaches, best in the morning before the afternoon sea breeze gets going. That same breeze is heaven for windsurfers and Leighton is a good spot for it. It's worth coming here on a windy day to watch the rainbow-coloured sails skimming across the sea.

Fremantle listings

For Sleeping and Eating price codes and other relevant information, see pages 10-14.

🌐 Sleeping

Fremantle *p60, map p62*
See Bars and clubs for pub accommodation.
$$$$ Esplanade, corner of Marine Terr and Essex St, T9432 4000 and T1800 998201, www.esplanadehotelfremantle.com.au. Freo's flagship, an elegant Federation hotel that has been the automatic choice for many visitors for over a century. Facilities include 3 courtyard pools with spa, sauna, smorgasbord, à la carte and buffet restaurants, fitness centre and bike hire. Many of the 300 rooms have access to the balconies. Internet available and free parking if you book directly online.
$$-$ Backpackers Inn YHA, 11 Packenham St, T9431 7065. Has 41 rooms and good facilities including internet access and large, well-equipped kitchen. En suite doubles and dorms (single sex or mixed).
$$-$ Old Firestation, 18 Phillimore St, T9430 5454, www.old-firestation.net. Has a laid-back atmosphere and lots of freebies, including off-street parking and internet. Dorms can be large, ranging from 4-15 people. It has an alcohol licence and well-equipped kitchen. It is also good at tracking down employment and has cheap curries for residents downstairs at **Bengal**. 24-hr reception,

late check-in can be arranged by phone.
$$-$ Sundancer, 80 High St, T9336 6080, www.sundancerbackpackers.com. The best of the big hostels and very well positioned. Rooms and communal facilities are bright and clean, the big kitchen is well-equipped and there is a sunny rear courtyard with pool. Free internet, a licensed bar and bike hire. 24-hr reception and check-in. Parking. Recommended.

B&Bs
If you're looking for a heritage B&B you're going to be spoilt for choice and the following are just a selection. All have friendly hosts who serve up excellent breakfasts. Most, however, do not have parking facilities.
$$$$-$$$ Terrace Central, 79-85 South Terr, T9335 6600, www.terracecentral.com.au. Bright and breezily decorated 1890s cottage (with extension) offering apartments, spacious doubles, twin and executive rooms. All have a/c, TVs and are en suite. Free Wi-Fi and off-street parking available. Continental breakfast included with the B&B rooms. Some rooms come with a 2-night minimum stay.
$$$ Fothergills, 20 Ord St, T9335 6784, www.babs.com.au/fothergills. Large, stately colonial house with 6 spacious en suite rooms, subdued but luxurious, and a very pleasant upstairs balcony. Breakfast in a

sunny conservatory. Some parking. Wi-Fi access available.

$$$ Port Mill, 17 Essex St, T9433 3832, www.babs.com.au/portmill. The white-washed rough stone walls and tight cottagey staircase make it hard to believe this new building isn't just as old as the 1863 flour mill opposite. 3 bright en suite rooms with balconies; the front 2 have great views. Continental breakfast to be enjoyed in the room included in the tariff.

Self-contained
$$$$ Quest Harbour Village, Mews Rd, Challenger Harbour, T9430 3888, www.quest harbourvillage.com.au. Modern, luxury apartments perched in a great spot between Challenger and Fishing Boat harbours. Parking and internet access available.
$$$ Westerley, 1A Tuckfield St, T9430 4458, www.westerley.com.au. A number of comfortable and centrally located properties including studios, converted warehouse, town houses and harbourside apartments. Free Wi-Fi available at most properties.

Caravan parks
$$$-$$ Coogee Beach, Cockburn Rd, 4 km south of town, T9418 1810 and T1800 817016. With direct beach access, BBQ, camp kitchens, motel and en suite cabins, tent sites.
$$$-$ Fremantle Village, 25 Cockburn Rd, 3 km south of the city centre on the coast road, T9430 4866, www.fremantlevillage.com.au. Village facilities include camp kitchens, Wi-Fi and broadband internet, laundry facilities and free gas BBQs. Motel units, cabins and chalets as well as en suite caravan sites and normal tent sites. No pets allowed.

🍴 Eating

Fremantle *p60, map p62*
The choice in Fremantle is staggering and it's a favourite eating destination for those who live in Perth. With its sunny climate, almost every restaurant and café has outdoor or pavement tables and many have been built to open onto the street so that they barely seem to have walls at all. The city's large Italian population has helped to build a very continental culture of coffee drinking, posing and long, leisurely hours of eating. Italian food and seafood predominate, but there are few Asian flavours here, too. The main eating areas are South Terr and around the Boat Harbour. It is said that it's hard to find a bad meal in Freo, and the following does not even begin to exhaust the possibilities.

$$$ Mussel Bar, 42 Mews Rd, T9433 1800, www.musselbar.com.au. Mon 1800-2200, Tue-Sun 1200-2200. Large, contemporary dining room with sloping glass windows looking out over the harbour, giving it the feel of a ship's wheelhouse. Excellent mussels, but also a range of seafood and grills.
$$$ Red Herring, 26 Riverside Rd, East Fremantle, T9339 1611, www.redherring. com.au. Daily 1200-1500 and 1700-2300, Sun also for breakfast 0800-1100. Considered one of the best seafood restaurants in Perth and running out of wall space for its awards, this contemporary restaurant sits on pylons over the river. Central sushi and oyster bar makes for a terrific appetizer. Save room for the fine dessert and cheese menu. Excellent wine list and wine-matching suggestions. Best to book in advance.
$$$-$ Capri, 21 South Terr, T9335 1399. Open 1200-1400, 1700-2130. This is the real thing: classic old-fashioned Italian cooking in a simple wood-panelled room. No fuss, no frills but wonderful flavours. Many seafood dishes. Unlicensed. BYO.
$$$-$ Left Bank, 15 Riverside Rd, East Fremantle, T9319 1315, www.leftbank.com.au. Café daily from 0700, restaurant Mon-Sat from 1200. A large, open pub on the river that concentrates on its food. Café-style menu downstairs with burgers and salads and very popular breakfasts, go early at the weekend. Classy mid-range restaurant upstairs with some romantic balcony tables. One of the

more popular spots for the traditional Perth Sun session.

$$-$ Maya Indian, 75-77 Market St, T9335 2796, www.mayarestaurant.com.au. Dinner Tue-Sun 1800-2200. Fri lunch 1200-1430. The authentic Indian food has won many awards and it's always busy. A short, traditional menu, fully licensed. Also offers regional tasting menus for parties of 4-people or more. Takeaway available.

$$-$ Pizza Bella Roma, 14 South Terr, T9335 1554. Tue-Thu 1700-late, Fri-Sun 1200-late. The best pizza and chilli mussels in an unpretentious setting. Licensed and BYO.

$ Cicerellos, 44 Mews Rd, on the harbour itself, T9335 1911, www.cicerellos.com.au. Open 1000-late. A dominating boatshed-style building that serves up portions of fish and chips to hundreds of tourists every day.

$ Kailis, 46 Mews Rd, T9335 7755, www.kailis.com. Massive boatshed-style building, similar to **Cicerellos**, also serving fish and chips.

$ Old Shanghai Food Court, 4 Henderon St, next to the **Sail & Anchor**. Wed-Thu 0930-2100, Fri-Sun 1000-2130. Good food from Japanese to juices and lots of pavement tables in the mall. Dead cheap.

$ Pizza On High 33 High St, T9335 4234. Lunch Mon-Fri 1100-1500, Dinner Wed-Sat 1730-late. Offering an all-you-can-eat 4 nights of the week, and BYO. The lunch specials are good value and takeaway is available.

$ Sweetlips, 47 Mews Rd, T9430 6902, www.sweetlips.com.au. Mon-Thu 1000-2030, Fri-Sun 1000-2100. A little further away from the harbour, behind **McDonalds**. Away from the crowds, offers good range of fish and chips. Café enclosed.

$ Vivisen Teahouse, 15 Point St, T9336 6699, www.vivisenteahouse.com. Daily 1100-1500, 1700-2200. Chinese restaurant offering a wide range of options, including home-made Dim Sum. Visitors should try the house special, Goji tea. BYO.

Cafés

There are dozens of cafés in and around Fremantle, and most can be relied upon for great coffee and service.

Fremantle Arts Centre, see Sights, page 64. A peaceful café, great for coffee or lunch.

Ginos, 1 South Terr, T9336 1464, www.ginoscafe.com.au. Daily 0700-2230. One of the original Italian cafés, **Ginos** has stuck to its simple formula of fast, honest Italian food, great coffee and friendly service. Order at the counter.

🎵 Bars and clubs

Fremantle *p60, map p62*
Note that dress codes and restrictions may apply at most venues, especially at night.

Clancy's Fish Pub, 51 Cantonment St, T9335 1351, www.clancysfishpub.com.au. Mon-Sat 1200-2400, Sun 1200-2200. A bit out of the way but one of the most relaxed pubs in Freo, Clancy's has a funky, alternative feel and great food available all day (Sun-Thu 1200-2100, Fri-Sat 1200-2130). The menu concentrates on fish and seafood but pasta, noodles and cakes are also on offer. The veranda is a fine place for a quiet drink. Entertainment and live music almost every day. Always packed for the Sun session. Recommended.

Little Creatures, 40 Mews Rd, T9430 5555, www.littlecreatures.com.au. Brewery Mon-Fri 1000-2400, Sat-Sun 0900-2400. A former boatshed and crocodile farm, now a cool, cavernous brewery and bar with a spacious veranda and boccia pitch. Excellent, inventive cheap food, including wood-fired pizzas, mussels and tapas, available all day. Laid-back atmosphere and friendly service. Quiz on Thu nights. **Creatures Loft** upstairs plays host to live bands and the occasional film night and is open Thu-Sun.

The Monk, 33 South Terr, T9336 3100, www.madmonk.com.au. Open 1100-2300. A microbrewery offering up porter, pale ale and bitter, amongst others, and tips on which will best complement your food. Wine and the occasional cider are available for the non-beer drinkers. A wide range of tapas dishes as well as pizzas and more hearty dishes. The terrace area is good for people watching.

Newport, 2 South Terr, T9335 2428, www.thenewport.com. Mon-Thu 1200-2400, Fri-Sat 1200-0100, Sun 1200-2200. A lively, relaxed pub smartened up with polished floors and aluminium chairs. Pool tables, atrium courtyard, dedicated room DJs who play every night. Backpacker and student night is Wed.

Norfolk, corner of Norfolk St and South Terr, T9335 5405, www.norfolkhotel.com.au. A social pub with a great enclosed stone courtyard, huge on Sun afternoons. Live music Thu-Sat in the Basement Lounge. Bar food available 1200-2100. The 9 rooms are some of the towns best pub options (**B-C**), those with shared facilities are cheaper.

Rosie O'Gradys, 23 William St, T9335 1645, www.rosieogradys.com.au. Pleasant, airy and spacious Irish theme pub (a chain). The walls and slate floors are green, of course, but the heritage building has been cleverly converted to Australian-style drinking rather than dark and cosy Irish-style. Cheap and hearty food (daily 1100-1500 and 1700-2100) and 17 bland but comfortable hotel rooms (**B-C**). Live music and entertainment every night.

Sail & Anchor, 64 South Terr, T9431 1666, www.sailandanchor.com.au. The pub that started the boutique beer and good food revolution in Freo around the time of the Americas Cup. The pub has a microbrewery producing many of the beers sold on site. The bistro does wood-fired pizzas, steaks and light meals. There is a lounge bar upstairs open at weekends. Also a good bottle shop. Brewery tours by appointment.

Clubs

Although Fremantle is not the automatic choice for clubbers there are a couple of options. Try **Kulcha**, www.kulcha.com.au, 13 South Terr, or **Metropolis**, www.metropolis fremantle.com.au, 58 South Terr.

⚙ Entertainment

Fremantle *p60, map p62*
Cinema
Luna on SX, 13 Essex St, T9430 5999, www.lunapalace.com.au. Fremantle's grooviest cinema, with discounts for students and YHA members.

Theatre
Deckchair Theatre, Victoria Hall, 179 High St, T9430 4771, www.deckchairtheatre.com.au. Puts on contemporary, home-grown productions, often with a Fremantle or multicultural theme.
Spare Parts Puppet Theatre, 1 Short St, T9335 5044, www.sppt.asn.au. Produces inventive children's entertainment.

⚙ Festivals and events

Fremantle *p60, map p62*
For more detailed information on festivals in Fremantle, visit www.fremantlefestivals.com.
Mar/Apr The **Street Arts Festival**, held every Easter, is Australia's biggest street performance festival and features artists from all over the world.
Mid-Nov The **Fremantle Festival** is held annually at various venues around the city. Over 120,000 people flock to the city to see and participate in dozens of events featuring local and world music, dance, acrobatics and art. Contact the City of Fremantle T9432 9888.

⚙ Shopping

Fremantle *p60, map p62*
There's some excellent shopping in the port city. Although the major chains are here, in or around High St Mall, there are also many quirky and interesting shops that help to give Fremantle its character. Fremantle shopping

hours are generally 0900-1700 with the exception of late-night shopping on Fri until 2100. Most shops are also open at the weekend. The **Fremantle Markets** are the best in WA, still held in the original Victorian market hall. The markets have a fresh fruit and vegetable section and sell clothes, jewellery, art and a whole host other items. The Henderson Mall entrance leads to shops selling wonderful fresh food such as bread, cheese and fish, so it's a good place to stock up for a picnic. Open Fri 1000-2000, Sat-Sun and public holiday Mon 1000-1800. The **E Shed Markets**, T9430 6393, www.eshed markets.com.au, do not match up to this high standard, but still have a few jewellery, clothes and craft shops that are worth a look if you're waiting for a ferry. Open Fri-Sun 0900-1730, food court and cafés to 2000.

Arts and crafts
Bead Post, 3/13 Market St, T9335 3936, www.thebeadpost.com.au. Beads and beading accessories. Offers jewellery repair services, as well as classes and workshops.
Creative Native, 65 High St. Mon-Fri 0900-1700, Sat 1000-1700 and Sun 1100-1700. One of several indigenous art shops on this strip. Aimed more at the casual tourist than the serious art buyer.
Didgeridoo Breath, 6 Market St, T9430 6009, www.didgeridoobreath.com. A good range of didgeridoos and they will teach you to play for free. There's also the option of shipping your purchase home.
Fremantle Arts Centre, 1 Finnerty St, T9432 9569. Excellent-quality craft work (ceramics, wood, textiles, jewellery) by WA artists at very reasonable prices.
Japingka, 47 High St, T9335 8265, www.japingka.com.au. Authentic high-quality Aboriginal art, sculpture and craftwork.

Bookshops
Chart and Map Shop, 14 Collie St, T9335 8665, www.chartandmapshop.com.au.

Mon-Fri 0900-1700, Sat 00900-1600 and Sun 1000-1600. For maps and guides check out their excellent range.
Elizabeth's Second-hand Bookshop, there are a number of branches of this excellent second-hand shop in Fremantle, including Street Mall, T9430 6700, and 8 South Terr, T9433 1310.
New Edition, 82 High St, T9335 2383. Sun-Thu 0900-1930 and Fri-Sat 0900-2130. One of Freo's best-loved shops in the heart of the cappuccino strip. Fantastic range of literature, art, travel and design books and an atmosphere conducive to hours of browsing. Fi & co also have a small boutique at the back selling clothes and accessories.

Clothing and jewellery
There are a few cutting-edge fashion boutiques in Market St.
Jalfreezi, South Terr Piazza, T9433 3340. A good range of attractive and cheap Indian clothing. Also visit the Fremantle Markets for this kind of clothing.
Zingara, Fremantle Markets (opposite the Market Bar). High-quality silver jewellery.

Food
The first stop has to be the markets, but failing that these are good options.
The Fremantle Bakehouse, 52 South Terr, T9430 9592, www.fremantlebakehouse. com.au. Stop at this busy café and bakery to sample some tasty fresh breads and pastries.
Kakulas Sister, 29-31 Market St, T9430 4445, www.kakulassister.com.au. Sells delicatessen foods and Italian groceries.
Woolstore Shopping Centre, 28 Cantonment St. Mon-Fri 0800-2100, Sat 0800-1700 and Sun 1200-1700. For general needs; houses a Coles, a pharmacy, etc.

Music
Record Finder, 87 High St. Daily Mon-Sat 1000-1700, Sun 1100-1700. A large affair with a huge stock of vinyl.

Outdoor equipment

Mountain Designs, Shop 3 Queensgate Centre, William St, T9335 1431, www.mountaindesigns.com. Head to this well-known and helpful chain store for all your outdoor needs.

⛰ Activities and tours

Fremantle *p60, map p62*
Boat cruises
See also Sailing, below.
Captain Cook Cruises, T9325 3341, www.captaincookcruises.com.au. Runs several cruises from East St Jetty. These include daily cruises to Perth (90 mins), Swan River scenic cruises (4 hrs), lunch cruises (3 hrs) and dinner cruises (4 hrs).
Rottnest Express, T1300 467688, www.rottnestexpress.com.au. Offers daily (in summer) Swan River Cruises that include morning tea and a full commentary. Whale-watching tours in season (Sep-Nov) cost about $50.

Diving
Australian Diving Academy, T9356 9577, www.ausdiving.com.au. Runs PADI courses and dive trips to Rottnest for $210. Meals are included on trips.
Dolphin Dive, 1 Cantonment St, T9336 6286, www.dolphindiveshop.com. Organizes several boat dives, including wreck and night dives, and has hire facilities. PADI courses are also offered. A Rottnest double dive with equipment costs $185.

Golf
Fremantle Public Golf Course, Montreal St, T9336 3933. Daily 0530-1900. Green fees are: $15 for 9 holes, $22 for 18 holes. Equipment hire available and there's also a driving range.

Parasailing
Westcoast Parasail, Mews Rd, Fishing Boat Harbour, T0417 188502, www.westcoast parasail.com.au. $75 for a single, $120 for a tandem jump.

Sailing
Leeuwin Ocean Adventure Foundation, B Berth, Victoria Quay, T9430 4105, www.sailleeuwin.com. Fremantle's resident tall ship, a magnificent 3-masted vessel that dominates Victoria Quay when it is moored there. It sails out on a variety of trips depending on the season. In summer it is based in the port and there are plenty of opportunities to get aboard for a day sail, mostly at weekends. Most trips last around 3 hrs and cost $95, children $60. Longer sailing trips are also available.

Tour operators
Fremantle Tram Tours, T9433 6674, www.fremantletrams.com.au. Trundle around Fremantle on their buses-dressed-as-trams on a hop-on hop-off service. The tour takes in Victoria Quay, Fremantle Prison, Arts Centre, Fishing Boat Harbour, Esplanade Hotel, Town Hall ($22, children $5, concessions $18). Longer tours also on offer. On Fri nights at 1845 there is a Ghostly Tram Tour, which includes torchlight tours of the Prison, Arts Centre and The Round House. Fish and chip dinner is included in the price ($60, children $45).

⊖ Transport

Fremantle *p60, map p62*
See also Activities and tours for transport around Fremantle. For more information , T136213 or www.transperth.wa.gov.au.

Air
Light aircraft from Jandakot Airport, east of Fremantle, take passengers to **Rottnest Island**, see page 72.

Bicycle/scooter
Fleet Cycles, 66 Adelaide St, T9430 5414, www.fleetcycles.com.au. Mon-Fri 0900-

1730, Sat 1000-1700, Sun 1100-1700.
Hires out bicycles.
Scoot Freo, 2 Phillimore St, T9336 5933,
www.scootfreo.com.au. Mon-Fri 1000-1600,
Sat-Sun 0900-1700. Hires out scooters and
3-wheel, 2-person scootcars. Closed if wet.

Bus
The main bus terminal is in front of the
railway station.

Selected bus services from Fremantle:
Booragoon, **City Busport**, **East Perth**,
105; **City Busport**, **East Perth** (from Queen
St), 106, 111; **Cottesloe**, **Stirling Highway**,
Kings Park, **St Georges Terr**, 103, 104;
Cottesloe, **Claremont**, 70; **Port Beach**,
Cottesloe Beach, **Scarborough**, 381
(weekdays); **Port Beach**, **Cottesloe Beach**,
Scarborough, **Hillarys**, 582 (weekends
only during Oct-Apr); **Rockingham Bus
Station**, 126 (weekdays only), 920.

Car hire
Ace, T9472 4222, www.acerent.com.au.
M2000, T9438 2828, www.m2000car.com.au.

Ferry
Fremantle presents the cheapest options for
getting to **Rottnest**. Oceanic Cruises, T9335
2666, www.oceaniccruises.com.au, and
Rottnest Express, T9335 6406,
www.rottnestexpress.com.au, both offer
services daily from C-Shed, near the railway
station ($59.50 day return). The latter also has
several ferry/hotel packages worth looking at
and both can arrange bike hire packages. For
those who want to reach Rottnest that bit

quicker, Rottnest Express also runs the *Mega
Blast*, Sep-May Thu-Mon 0925, returns 1645,
It's the same price as the ferry and is great
fun, there are splash jackets available and you
may want one if you're sitting at the front.

Taxi
There is a supervised taxi rank on South Terr,
near Fremantle Markets, Fri-Sat 2300-0500.
Swan, T131330, **Black & White**, T131008,
www.blackandwhitecabs.com.au. From
Perth a journey costs $40-45.

Train
The Fremantle Line runs between Perth
and Fremantle via **Subiaco**, **Claremont**
and **Cottesloe**. Services are every 10-15 mins
0530-1930 and every 30-60 mins 1900-0230.
Sat services are at similar times running
0600-0230 and Sun 0730-2330. The
journey takes about 30 mins in total.

❸ Directory

Fremantle *p60, map p62*
Banks ATMs for major banks on Adelaide St
between Point and Queen Sts. **Interforex**,
next to VIC, 0800-1930. **Internet** Travel
Lounge, 16 Market St, Mon-Fri 0800-2000,
Sat-Sun 1000-1800. **Library** 8 William St,
T9432 9766. Mon and Fri 0930-1730,
0930-1720, Tue-Thu 0930-2000, Sat
0930-1700. **Medical services** Fremantle
Hospital, corner of Alma St and South Terr,
T9431 3333. **Police** 45 Henderson St, T9430
1222. **Post** 13 Market St, T9239 7600,
Mon-Fri 0900-1700.

Rottnest Island

Rotto, as the locals call it, once a penal settlement, is now Perth's holiday playground. Just 20 km west of the city, it feels a long way from the metropolitan commotion. Generations of Perth families have come to frolic here every summer and it's a traditional place to celebrate the end of school, university or parental control. The entire coast is one long cordon of quite magical sandy bays and clear aquamarine water and so, understandably, come summer, many beaches get very busy. However, even at this time, you'll find almost deserted stretches towards the western and southern parts of the island. The offshore reefs are full of brightly coloured fish, exotic corals and limestone caves, and littered with wrecks. The island itself is 11 km long and 4 km wide and covered in low bushy scrub with some patches of eucalypt woodland. Much of this provides cover for the island's famous small wallaby, the quokka, after which the island was dubiously named. There are few permanent human residents as the island is carefully managed to preserve the environment and scarce water resources. The number of overnight visitors is kept to a sustainable level and cars are not allowed.

Ins and outs ▸▸ *For listings, see pages 74-77.*

Getting there There are two ways of getting to Rotto: by air (from Jandakot Airport) and ferry. The cheapest way is to take public transport to Fremantle and take a ferry from there. ▸▸ *See Transport, page 25, and under the relevant departure point.*

Getting around As only essential service vehicles and buses are allowed on the island, there are just two principal choices if you want to see more of the island than Thomson Bay Settlement: bikes and buses. There is a free shuttle bus that operates between the main accommodation areas on the island. It leaves from the main bus stop in Thomson Bay, travels to Geordie Bay Store for Geordie, Fay's and Longreach Bays, then returns to the main bus stop before heading to the airport and Kingstown Barracks. The **Bayseeker** bus travels clockwise right around the coast road, but doesn't get out to the West End. It operates a jump-on, jump-off system with 18 stops on the circuit and goes every 30-60 minutes. A day fare is $12, children $5.50, concessions $10. Services run 0830-1630. There is also a train service going to and from the south end of the Settlement and Oliver Hill lookout; fares includes a tour at Oliver Hill, except for the last ride of the day. Two-hour round trips hourly 1030-1430 in summer, 1230-1430 in winter. Tickets $25, children $15, concessions $20, available from the VIC.

Tourist information VIC ① *Thomson Bay Settlement, T9372 9732, Sat-Thu 0730-1700, Fri 0730-1930.* Also in Thomson Bay is a small shopping mall with a post office, ATM, takeaways, general store, bakery and clothes/gift shops. The general store stocks books and has a bottle shop. It also offers a free delivery service to the island's accommodation from 0800-1800. There is a similarly stocked store at Geordie Bay, where there's also a café serving light meals in peak season. Both open daily. There is a **Wellness Centre** near the mall, which offers beauty treatments as well as being home to the island's pharmacy. The island has a nursing post, T9292 5030, police station, T131 444, and ranger's office, T9372 9788. See also www.rottnestisland.com.

Background

Until 7000 years ago Rottnest was a peninsula, attached to the mainland. Since the connecting bridge drowned, a result of the ending of the last ice age, the island was abandoned by any Aboriginals who may have been living there and the new island christened *Wadjemup* by the mainland local peoples. In 1696 the island was first visited by Europeans in a Dutch vessel commanded by Willem de Vlamingh. Seeing the island swarming with the small wallabies, the Dutch considered the island a rat's nest and named it accordingly. As well as the quokkas, as they are known to the Noongar, the island is home to a variety of animals and flora marooned when the island was cut off. The fact that it was an island close to a European colony doomed it to become a penal settlement, but this time with a difference. A few convicts were shipped over, but for the most part it was used to imprison Aboriginal criminals who incurred the authority's displeasure on the mainland. Many of the buildings constructed for this purpose still remain in and around the island's only village, known simply as the Settlement. For the last 80 or so years the island has served a dual purpose as holiday destination and military encampment, with the latter moving out in the 1980s.

Sights

While **Thomson Bay Settlement** has the ferry terminal, is the main settlement and has most of the island's services, it is also something of an open-air museum, and the general layout is claimed to be Australia's oldest intact streetscape. Most interesting is the part of the Lodge known as the **Quod**, and the heritage precinct in front of it. Once one of the most feared places on the island, it was built in 1838 to house dozens of Aboriginal criminals in horrendous conditions. There were still prisoners on the island when it was converted into a tourist hostel in 1911. Most of the current double rooms were once two cells holding about 10 men. The **museum and library** ① *museum daily 1045-1530, gold coin donation; library 1400-1545, free,* just behind the general store in the mall, are the main repositories of the islands history. Museum displays include the early days as a prison for Aboriginal men, island shipwrecks, military use and its development as Perth's holiday isle.

Also in Thomson Bay the original **Salt Store** has a small gallery where artists exhibit their work, and an exhibition that focuses on the island's early colonial history. This is also where the Rottnest Volunteer Guides can be found, and where a number of free guided tours depart from. Further afield there is an interesting walk south through the dunes at Kingstown Barracks to the **Bickley Battery**. The 45-minute stroll takes you past several ruined buildings that were once gun emplacements, built in the 1930s to defend Perth against any interlopers. Almost in the centre of the island is **Oliver Hill** ① *tours on the hour*

1000-1400, Apr-Jun, $7, children $3, concessions $5, or included in cost of the train from Thomson Bay, 1 hr to walk, 30 mins to cycle, used during the Second World War as another gun emplacement. Underground is a small maze of tunnels. The nearby **Wadjemup Lighthouse** ⓘ *T9372 9732, $7, children $3, concessions $5*, built in 1896, is accessible to visitors and tours run every 30 minutes 1100-1430. The 360-degree views over Rottnest Island are outstanding. The island's second lighthouse, **Bathurst**, is nearer to Thomson Bay and was built in 1900 to support Wadjemup following the City of York shipping disaster in 1899. It is not open to the public, although the Volunteer Guides do run a free walk up to the lighthouse during which they tell of the exploits of the pilots (experienced sailors who guided ships around the dangerous reefs) and crew on Rottnest.

Beaches are what Rottnest is all about for most visitors. There are over a dozen picture-postcard bays with white-sand beaches and usually clear, intensely blue water. Reefs lie just offshore from some beaches and many are enclosed by dramatic limestone headlands. The most sheltered are along the north shore and these also get the busiest, especially the **Basin**, the most picturesque bay on the island. The Basin has covered picnic tables and toilets, adding to its popularity. Other small bays a bit further from Thomson Bay include **Little Armstrong** on the north shore and **Little Salmon** on the south. The water can get choppy in the afternoons at the latter. **Longreach** and **Geordie** are long sweeping bays overlooked by accommodation and often crowded with boats. **Salmon Bay** in the south is of a similar scale, clear of boats and can be good for boogie boarding, though there are no facilities.

Diving and **snorkelling** is excellent off Rottnest, with a large variety of wrecks, fish, corals and limestone caves. Particularly good snorkelling spots can be found off Parker Point, where there is a marked out trail, Little Salmon Bay, parts of Salmon Bay and the Basin. **Surfing** is best at Strickland, Salmon and Stark Bays.

Rottnest Island listings

For Sleeping and Eating price codes and other relevant information, see pages 10-14.

🛏 Sleeping

Most of the accommodation on the island is in self-contained cottages, villas or cabins. There is also a youth hostel, which operates out of Kingstown Barracks, and camping. All need to be booked through the **Accommodation Office**, T1800 111111 or T9432 9111, reservations@rottnestisland.com, Mon-Sat 0830-1700.

Thomson Bay has the most self-catering accommodation and accordingly has a resort feel about it. There are also options at the former military Kingstown Barracks, and also at Geordie Bay on the north coast. During the Dec-Jan summer period it is virtually impossible to find a room, cabin or space to pitch your tent unless you've booked it months in advance. Even outside of this period weekends commonly see the island booked almost full, so either book well ahead or plan for a mid-week visit. During peak WA school holidays a ballot system is used to allow visitors equal chances of reserving accommodation. You need to enter the ballot if you wish to book accommodation for these specific periods. See www.rottnestisland.com for more information. Some of the ferry companies offer ferry/accommodation/bike packages that may shave a few dollars off the cost. **$$$$ Hotel Rottnest**, Bedford Av, Thomson Bay, T9292 5011, www.hotelrottnest.com.au. Converted from a former residence for the Western Australian governor, it has a dozen fully serviced motel-style rooms with private

Quokka spotting

When the Dutch explorer Willem Vlamingh encountered Rottnest Island he encumbered it with a name that suggests the opposite of its natural beauty. In Dutch Rottnest means 'rat nest'. Europeans simply had no language to describe the unique Australian fauna. The 'rats' Vlamingh saw were the small wallabies (*Setonix bracyurus*), which still populate the island. Now commonly known as the quokka, from the Noongar word, these appealing wallabies are about 30 cm high. Although most closely identified with the island, the habitat of quokkas actually spreads along the southwestern coastal region. However, on the mainland they have become endangered due to predation by foxes and habitat loss. There are a few left in Dwellingup, the Stirling Ranges and on Bald Island, but Rottnest is the last bastion of a sizeable population, with about 8000-10,000. Even so, they suffer in summer because freshwater supplies are much lower than they were before settlement. Constant interaction with people, to their detriment, has also made some of them quite tame so you have a very good chance of seeing them. Visitors are now asked not to touch or feed them. If you're not venturing beyond the settlements you should always be able to find them hanging around the shop at Geordie Bay, alongside the Garden Lake boardwalk behind the Lodge, and at the short boardwalk opposite the turn-off to Kingstown Barracks.

bathrooms, mostly around an adjacent courtyard, but some overlooking the bay (these are more expensive). The rooms are pricey for what they are, and there's no breakfast included, but the hotel is very near the restaurants and the jetty. There is a bar and restaurant, with a wide selection of wines and beers.

$$$$ Rottnest Lodge, Kitson St, Thomson Bay, T9292 5161, www.rottnestlodge.com.au. The island's premier establishment, which incorporates many of the early colonial prison buildings, including the Quod. Rooms are furnished in contemporary style and most face onto a courtyard, the pool or the Quod. A few face a lake, but this can smell a little in high summer. All rooms en suite and continental breakfast is included. Other facilities include a licensed restaurant, pub and a cocktail bar.

Self-contained

There is a wide choice of accommodation on the island, almost all around the eastern bays, ranging from beautifully renovated colonial cottages to small huts. Each is reasonably well equipped, and you just need to bring sheets and pillowcases. In size most range from 4 to 8 beds, though there are a few larger ones around Kingstown Barracks (up to 18 beds). Of the hundreds available the following represent a few of the best options. Prices drop considerably if you're staying n 1 night. At certain times of year, however, principally school holidays, the demand for accommodation is such that it is allocated by ballot about 6 months beforehand. Ballot application forms can be found on the Rottnest website. Kingstown is, strictly speaking, an alcohol-free area. Bookings for all these are through the Accommodation Office up to a year in advance.

$$$$ Commander's House, more isolated than most in an inland position, but with fine views down across the ocean.

$$$$ Lighthouse Keeper's Cottages (villas 547 and 548), www.lighthouse.net.au, are in a wonderful shore-side spot next to Bathurst Lighthouse, with front verandas looking across to Perth. Slightly cheaper than **Commander's House**. Linen provided, book well in advance. Recommended.

$$$ Geordie Bay, modern, villas all have good views across the bay and immediate access to the beach.

$$ Caroline Thomson, the best budget option, 1 room cabins with kitchenette and bathroom in Thomson Bay.

Camping

There is a small area set aside for camping in Thomson Bay it is not allowed over the rest of the island. Adults $10 per night.

The **Allison Camping Area** has fresh water and gas BBQ facilities but it is unpowered. Booking sites in peak times is as necessary as booking cabins and villas, and can be done through the Accommodation Office. The camping area is an alcohol-free zone.

🍴 Eating

$$$-$ Aristos, just along from **Dtme**, the long boardwalk also looks out over the harbour, T9292 5171, www.aristosrottnest.com.au. Mon-Fri 1000-2000, Sat-Sun 1000-2030 (coffee and cakes from 1000, lunch from 1130 every day). A chain eatery offering fish and chips, oysters, chilli mussels, lobster, chowder and seafood platters. All served up with great views of the ocean. Coffee and cake is served all day and there are bacon and egg rolls on the breakfast menu.

$$$-$ Hotel Rottnest, see Sleeping. Offers old favourites such as burgers, seafood dishes, pizzas, salads and steak. Food from 1100-2030. There is a large ocean-front bar and seating area, and live music on Sat nights.

$$$-$ Rottnest Lodge, see Sleeping. **Marlins Restaurant** is surprisingly reasonably priced given its decidedly upmarket feel. The evening à la carte menu (1800-2100) is slightly pricier than lunch, but the food is the best on the island. The **Governor's Bar** serves pub grub.

$$ Dtme, central to Thomson's Bay with terrace views over the harbour, T9292 5286, Open 0700-2100. Part of the gallic-style chain. Simple meals from Thai chicken curries to steak and Guinness pies. The place gets very busy but there are no bookings.

⛰ Activities and tours

Rottnest Island *p72*
Boat and kayak tours
Rottnest Adventure Centre, Henderson Av, T9292 5292. Rents out kayaks (double for $50, single $30 for 2 hrs), fishing and snorkelling gear, and bikes. Can also supply weight belts and tanks for those who are diving.

Rottnest Express, T1300 467688, www.rottnestexpress.com.au. Sep-Jun from Mon-Thu at 1100. Offers eco-adventure tours around the island, with commentary on the island's unique wildlife and geography. $50, children $25, concessions $45.

Underwater Explorer, T9292 5292. A large glass-bottomed boat that heads out several times a day on a variety of short cruises including a 45-min wreck and reef tour ($29, children $15, concessions $27), and longer snorkelling trips (1 hr, $39, children and concessions $35), equipment hire $15.

Cinema

The latest releases are shown at the **Rottnest Island Picture Hall**. Session times are posted outside or are available from the VIC. Make sure to check the **Transfer Bus** timetables, as some films finish after the last service. $10, children $8. Open all year.

Diving

As a rule of thumb the wind comes from the east in the morning and the southwest in the afternoon. Precisely where it is best to jump into the water around the island depends on the weather and prevalent wind direction. In general it is best to be in the lee of the wind, but before deciding where to head for have a chat with the VIC. There are plans to open a

Dive Centre behind **Dtme**, where it will be possible to hire equipment and re-fill tanks.

Dive operators in Perth (see page 54), Fremantle (see page 70) and even as far away as Rockingham (see page 106) and Busselton (see page) offer dive trips to Rottnest.

Golf and bowls
Golf and Country Club, Sommerville Dr, T9292 5105. Tue-Sat 0830-1100, 1400-1900 in summer, daily 0900-1630 in the main winter season. Has a 9-hole course and a bowling green. Club hire available.

Surfing
There are a few good breaks around the island, notably at Stark Bay, Strickland Bay, North Point and Salmon Point. Take note, these are all reef breaks and are not suitable for beginners.

Tennis
There are free tennis courts at Bathurst Point, Geordie Bay and Kingstown Barracks. Racket hire is available from **Rottnest Island Bike Hire** in Thomson Bay.

Tour operators
Discovery Tour, is a 1-hr coach tour which sets off around the island from Thomson Bay at 1120, 1340 and 1350, with full commentary on the human and natural history of the island. The tour includes visits to Wadjemup Lighthouse and the West End. Adults $32, children $15, concessions $25. Tickets can be bought at the VIC.
Rottnest Island Joyflights, T9292 5027 or T1800 500006, www.rottnest.de. Scenic flights operating from the airport. Minimum 2 passengers, operates on demand 1030-1530, $35 per person for 10 mins over the island, $85 per person for 35-min flights over Perth and $100 per person for a combination of the 2. **Rottnest Voluntary Guides**, T9372 9777.

Conduct guided walks daily around Thomson Bay, mostly focusing on the islands penitential and military history. In summer the programme is extended to include evening walks that include star-gazing and ghost stories. Gold coin donation appreciated, see VIC for current programme.

⊝ Transport

Rottnest Island *p72*
Air
Rottnest Air Taxi, T9292 5027 and T1800 500006, www.rottnest.de. Offers return trips from Jandakot Airport, east of Fremantle, anytime during daylight hours. Fares from $80 per person, depending on numbers ($150 return if there are just 2 of you). Once on the island they also offer quick scenic flights (see **Rottnest Island Joyflights**, above).

Bicycle
Bikes can be brought over on the ferries, and the ferry companies also offer bike hire packages. Hire on the island is from **Rottnest Bike Hire**, behind Rottnest Hotel, T9292 5105, which has a wide range to suit all ages including some tandems ($20-27, children $13.50-21, tandem $45 per day) and free electric beach wheelchairs. Open 0830-1700. It also offers a recovery service in case you suffer a flat tyre and need to be rescued. Beware, however, that the coast road around the island undulates over the dunes like a roller-coaster. The slopes may be short, but they are often quite steep and cycling is a tiring business, so avoid single speed bikes. Also note that there is no fresh water west of either Geordie Bay or Kingstown Barracks and you should take plenty to drink in summer.

Ferry
Ferries run to **Barrack Street Jetty** in **Perth**, the **C-Shed** in **Fremantle** and Hillarys. See the Transport sections at the departure point for details.

Swan Valley

The Swan Valley is Perth's wine region, just a 45-minute drive from the city. In truth it's half a valley, bordered to the east by the Darling Range, but running flat to the west all the way to the northern Perth suburbs. It was settled early in Perth's history and vines were being grown by 1836 at what is now Houghtons, the valley's best-known winery. All sorts of other fruit and vegetables are also grown here, and it seems that almost every other house has a sign outside advertising table grapes and rock melons. At the southern end of the valley is Guildford, an inland port established in 1829, but falling out of favour early in its history, which helped preserve many early Victorian buildings.

Ins and outs ⯈⯈ *For listings, see pages 81-83.*

Getting there and around Trains leave from East Perth station to Guildford and Midland, but this isn't the ideal way to tour the valley. Ideally you need your own transport, or to take a tour. A taxi to or from Perth airport costs $30, double that from Perth.

Tourist information The main **VIC** ① *on the corner of Meadow and Swan Sts, T9379 9400, www.swanvalley.com.au, 0900-1600*, for the region is in Guildford. The helpful staff will advise visitors on a route depending on what they'd like to taste (ie only sparkling wines).

Sights

Wineries

There are some 40 wineries in the region, ranging from one of the largest producers in the state to several one-person operations. Most offer wines in the $15-30 range. Cellar door hours vary widely, and Monday to Tuesday is probably the worst time to visit as some of the smaller wineries keep these as their days off. Many have cafés or restaurants, most of which have outdoor vine-covered courtyards. ⯈⯈ *See Eating, page 82.*

The following is only a small selection of the wineries operating in the Swan Valley, the route outlined below takes visitors on a circuit starting and finishing at the VIC. Travel north along West Swan Road to find **Sandalford** ① *3210 West Swan Rd, T9374 9374, www.sandalford.com, cellar door 1000-1700*, one of the two heavyweights in the valley offering an extensive range of wines. The 2005 Prendiville Reserve Cabernet Sauvignon is the specialty. Winery tours run from 1100-1500 and are rounded off with a full appreciation and tasting session ($22), and every Saturday (at 1100) you can become a winemaker for a day on a tour that includes an exclusive blending session and a set lunch ($125). Wines cost $14-90.

Little River ① *2 Forest Rd, T9296 4462, www.littleriverwinery.com, daily 1000-1700*, is signposted further up West Swan Road. Wines include the rare Viognier Marsanne and are priced $14-144. **Edgecombe Brothers** ① *Gnangara and West Swan Rds, T9296 4307, www.edgecombebrothers.com.au, daily 1000-1700*, is family-run and one of the most laid-back and welcoming wineries in the valley. Wines cost $18.50-68. The unpretentious shop sells an excellent range of home-produced jams, sauces and produce. The café serves breakfast, a simple light lunch using seasonal ingredients or cream tea. Try the famous Muscat ice cream.

As the West Swan Road merges with the Great Northern Highway head south again and turn off onto Memorial Avenue. Here visitors will find **Mann** ① *105 Memorial Av, T9296 4348, Aug-Dec Wed-Sun 1000-1700*, a one-man operation continuing three generations of expertise in producing a smooth, dry Mithode Champenoise. A bargain at $20. Jack Mann has also produced an entirely new variety of grape, the Cygneblanc, though the wine is a little pricier at $30. Also on Memorial Avenue is **Upper Reach** ① *Memorial Av, T9296 0078, www.upperreach.com.au, daily 1100-1700*, a friendly winery that produces some of the valley's finest wines, particularly their Shiraz and Chardonnay. Wines cost $15-30. They also rent out a fully self- contained 2-bedroom cottage with indoor spa and views of the vineyard (**LL-A**). Note Saturday night is only available as part of a two-night booking.

Lamonts ① *85 Bisdee Rd, T9296 4485, www.lamonts.com.au, Fri-Mon 1000-1700*, is a large family-run winery with well- respected wines costing $15-65. Light snacks can be enjoyed while wine tasting. From here re-join the Great Northern Highway until Barrett Street. **Sittella** ① *100 Barrett St, T9296 2600, www.sittella.com.au, Tue-Sun 1100-1600*, claims one of the valleys best views from its large covered wooden deck. The sparkling Chenin is a specialty. Wines cost $14-38. Winery tours by arrangement.

Houghton ① *Dale Rd, T9274 9540, www.houghton-wines.com.au, daily Sep- May 1000-1700, Jun-Aug 1000-1600*, is the valley's expansive elder statesman and produces some of the most popular wines in Australia. Wines cost $15-70. Its cheaper ranges, such as Houghton Stripe, are consistently good. It has a small museum, gallery, children's playground and simple café but the big draw is its long lawn dotted with tall jacaranda trees. Picnickers are welcome, though platters, ploughmans and pizzas are available daily for lunch.

Jane Brook ① *229 Toodyay Rd, T9274 1432, www.janebrook.com.au, daily 1000-1700*, is slightly set apart from the rest of the action. A family-run winery it has a large covered decking area devoted to serving up substantial gourmet platters. The Plain Jane range is good value at $15, while more traditional vintages go for $20-35.

Around the valley

The Swan Valley is not just a haven for wine buffs. If you're interested in early Perth history this is also a good place to trace some of the earliest developments in the colony. WA's oldest church, **All Saints**, was built on the furthest spot Captain Stirling reached in his exploration of 1827. The simple red-brick building, over 160 years old, is still in use today and is usually open to visitors.

The arts scene has been growing for some time and there are now a number of seriously exciting artists in the valley. Antonio Battistessa, the Wizard of Fire, has been creating ornate iron sculptures and furniture for years and his work can be found all over Perth. His studio, **Battistessa** ⓘ *corner of Campersic and Neuman Rds, T9296 4121, 0900-1600*, is continuously growing. **Maalinup** ⓘ *West Swan Rd, T9296 0711, www.maalimia.com.au, 1000-1700*, is an Aboriginal-owned and operated cultural centre with workshops and two galleries. The premier room exhibits a few fine original artworks, woodcarvings and didgeridoos, the other houses the more run-of-the-mill works found in many gift shops. Jude Taylor, the proprietor of **Jude Taylor Studio** ⓘ *510 Great Northern Highway, T9250 8838, www.taylorstudio.com.au, opening hours vary so call ahead*, can seemingly turn her hand to almost anything and the studio houses a brilliant collection of art, sculpture and furniture. There is also a nice little café where you can enjoy food and drinks indoors or on beautiful wooden furniture outdoors. **Lamonts winery** (see above) has a gallery featuring many local and WA artists.

The **Margaret River Chocolate Company** ⓘ *5123 West Swan Rd, T9250 1588, www.chocolatefactory.com.au, daily 0900-1700*, offers some sweet relief from wine and galleries. Housed in a smart building, it has a long counter in front of a huge wall of chocolate, within which is a window onto the chocolate-making activities beyond. The wide range of delicious chocs can be bought individually or by the bag, and there's a café (open 0900-1630).

Guildford

Guildford, 20 km from Perth, 16 km from Mundaring, retains many old buildings from its early founding as the agricultural base to supply the Swan River Colony, but as yet makes very little of them other than as accommodation. The **courthouse** and **gaol complex** ⓘ *corner of Swan and Meadow Sts, 0900-1600, $2*, dates back to 1841 and, as a museum, now has a collection of colonial memorabilia. Entry to these also includes a peek inside one of the original settlers' cottages, constructed around 1880. Next door is **Guildford Village Potters** ⓘ *22 Meadow St, T9279 9859, www.guildfordpotters.webs.com, Mon-Fri 0930-1500, Sat-Sun 1000-1630*, a commercial operation that displays work from over 20 local potters. On show is a wide range, mostly a mix of practical, rustic ceramics with some fairly esoteric decorative pieces.

Walyunga National Park
ⓘ *$11 per car.*
Some 15 km north of central Swan Valley, this 18-sq-km block sits on the western escarpment of the Darling Range at the point at which the Avon River winds its way through to the plains to the west. It's a river that draws many visitors, particularly during the **Avon Descent**, www.avondescent.com.au, in the first weekend in August when competitors brave the length of Syds Rapids in their race downstream. Permanent water and a good supply of native tucker also made this a fine spot for the areas first inhabitants and one of the park's shorter trails describes some of the local Aboriginal stories. There are two parking areas, both with toilets and wood-fired BBQs. The further of the two, adjacent to **Boongarup Pool**, tends to be the quieter and is closer to the rapids. Three longer circular bush walks head off from the car parks: the shortest is the **Kangaroo Trail**, taking about one hour; the longest, the **Echidna Trail**, takes about four hours. The latter reaches the highest point in the park (260 m) and you'll get views across the Avon Valley.

Whiteman Park

ⓘ T9209 6000, www.whitemanpark.com, Mon-Fri 0830-1800, Sat-Sun 0830-1900, entry via Lord St, where the No 336 Morley-Ellenbrook bus drops off, use the courtesy phone at the entrance building to arrange a pick-up.

Covering more than 3000 ha of natural and regenerated bush, Whiteman Park, 20 km from Perth, is the most family-orientated of Perth's peripheral parks, focusing on children's activities, picnic facilities and visitor attractions rather than extensive bushwalking. The park hosts equestrian and shooting centres but the main visitor area is at the **Village**, with extensive picnic facilities (and associated car parks) around nearby **Mussel Pool**, a small lake and area of wetland. The picnic facilities are impressive: dozens of gas-fired and wood-fired BBQs with firewood provided free. There are vast lawned areas and quite a few covered tables, some of which can be booked ahead. **Mussel Pool West** is home to the **Birds of Prey Flying Displays** ⓘ T0438 388383, Sat-Sun 1100 and 1430, weather permitting, $9, children $5, concessions $7, operated by the WA Birds of Prey Centre.

In the village are the **visitor centre** ⓘ Mon-Fri 0830-1700, Sat-Sun 1000-1600, café, a few craft shops, children's playground and pool, and the **Motor Museum of WA** ⓘ T9249 9457, 1000-1600, $8, children and concessions $5, which has the largest collection of vintage vehicles in the state. Adjacent is a separate **Tractor Museum** ⓘ T9209 3480, Wed, Sat and Sun 1000-1400, gold coin donation. Theres also a **Transport Heritage Centre** ⓘ trams/trains operate Tue, Thu, Fri, Sat and Sun 1100-1400, $5-8, children $2.50-4, where tourist trains and vintage trams snake through the bush and connect the village with Mussel Pool. Another attraction in the park is **Caversham Wildlife Park** ⓘ T9248 1984, www.cavershamwildlife.com.au, 0900-1730 (last entry 1630), $22, children $8. This park holds the largest collection of animals in the state. They have over 200 species of birds, mammals and reptiles from all over the country, and a few from overseas. Highlights include the wombats, some of which can be met and cuddled.

The **Whiteman Explorer** ⓘ T9209 6000, Mon 1100 and 1300, free, offers 45-minute guided tours of Whiteman Park in a restored vintage bus.

As well as the static attractions, Whiteman Park plays host to a series of regular child- and adult-orientated events, including concerts and funfairs.

Swan Valley listings

For Sleeping and Eating price codes and other relevant information, see pages 10-14.

☻ Sleeping

Swan Valley *p78*

$$$$ Swan Valley Oasis Resort, West Swan Rd, T9296 5500, www.swanvalleyoasis.com. Luxurious resort with 28 rooms, all have king-sized beds and there is also a self-contained 1-bedroom apartment with spa and balcony. The on-site restaurant is open for breakfast, lunch and dinner every day and home-brewed beer is served in the adjacent **Mash** Brewery, T9296 5588, www.mashbrewing. com.au. There is also a swimming pool and a golf course nearby.

$$$ Chapel Farm Getaways, 231 Toodyay Rd, T9250 4755, www.chapelfarmgetaways. com.au. 6 unusual en suite a/c rooms. Cooked breakfast included. Also outdoor pool, spa and licensed restaurant, Thu lunch, Fri-Sun lunch and dinner. It also does Mongolian BBQs on Fri and Sun. Recommended.

$$$ Settlers Rest Farmstay, George St, T/F9250 4540, www.settlersrest.com.au.

Historic, beautifully furnished 3-bedroom weatherboard cottage in a quiet, central spot. Open fires, a/c and traditional verandas. Minimum 2-night stay at weekends.

Caravan parks

$$$-$$ Swan Valley Tourist Park, West Swan Rd, T9274 2828. Small, homely campground with swimming pool, on-site vans and en suite cabins. In the middle of the wine region.

$$ Banksia Tourist Park, 219 Midland Rd, T9250 2398, www.banksiatourist.com.au. Self-contained units and en suite chalets.The excellent facilities include a swimming pool, a covered playground, a deli/café and internet access.

Guildford p80

$$$$-$$$ Rose & Crown, 105 Swan St, T9279 8444, www.rosecrown.com.au. This grand old coaching inn is officially the oldest pub in WA, and does indeed ooze its early colonial character. The 4 rooms upstairs are sumptuous, unashamedly old-worldly, but scale dramatically in price. Modern motel rooms also available. All rooms are en suite. Meals available include substantial breakfasts 0700-0900, simple cheap light lunches 1200-1500 and mid-range dinners from Mon-Sat 1800-2100.

$$$ The Hollies, 5 Water St, T9279 3641, www.thehollies.com.au. Separated from the main house, guests stay in the self- contained **Summer House**. Continental breakfast is included.

Swan Valley p78
Wineries and breweries

$$$ Sandalford, 3210 West Swan Rd, T9374 9374, www.sandalford.com. Daily 1200-1500. Delicious and filling food in a great location. The cuisine is Modern Australian with a strong Italian influence, and uses a lot of fresh, simple flavours. The cheese selection

will make any foodie happy.

$$$-$ Elmar's In the Valley, 3781 West Swan Rd, T9296 6354, www.elmars.com.au. Wed-Thu 1000-1700, Fri-Sun 1000-2200. A German microbrewery and restaurant. Schwarzbier and Pilsner are served up with hearty meals such as bratwurst, schnitzel and pork shank. There are also tasting plates, snacks and salads.

$$ Little River, 6 Forest Rd, T9296 4462. Fri-Wed 1030-1630. A little bit of rustic France in the Swan, both food and wine being strongly gallic influenced. Casual menu, cream teas, home-made desserts and ice creams. The duck confit is especially good.

$$ Sittella, 100 Barrett St, T9296 2600, www.sittella.com.au. Tue-Sun 1100-1600. Eat on the covered deck or inside the large, contemporary but earthy dining room. A la carte or set menus for lunch, with an emphasis on seafood. Recommended.

$$-$ Upper Reach, Memorial Av, T9296 0078, www.upperreach.com.au. Daily 1100-1700. This winery is in a very picturesque location and has a pleasant café that serves up a good snack and chat range, as well as more substantial dishes. It offers platters, good coffee and teas, but the real highlight is the extensive breakfast menu on Sun (0830-1000).

$ Jane Brook, 229 Toodyay Rd, T9274 1432, www.janebrook.com.au. Open 1000-1700. Famous for its summer gourmet platters, in winter it serves up very tasty home-made pies. There are other small snacks, cheeseboards and a dessert of the day. Afternoon teas are also served.

Around the valley
Taylors Art and Coffee House,

510 Great Northern Highway, T9250 8838, www.taylorstudio.com.au. Open for breakfast and lunch Wed-Sun 0900-1700. This pleasant café adjacent to the **Taylor Studio**, serves up excellent food. Friendly service and a beautifully designed setting make it the

perfect place to relax. Takeaway available. Recommended.

Guildford *p80*
$$$ Padburys Café Restaurant,
114 Terrace Rd, T9378 4484, www.padburys restaurant.com.au. Sat-Sun for breakfast 0830-1100 and Tue-Sun for lunch 1100-1500 and dinner 1700-late. Award-winning restaurant with a Modern Australian menu. Alfresco dining, fully licensed.

▲ Activities and tours

Swan Valley *p78*
Beer Nuts Brewery Tours, T9295 0605, www.beernuts.com.au. Tours around the Swan Valley's microbreweries for beer lovers. Visits include Elmar's in the Valley, Mash Brewing, Ironbark Brewery, The Feral Brewing Company, Duckstein Brewery and The Kimberley Rum Company from Thu-Sun. Tours range from those where you bring your own lunch ($70 per person for 3-8 people), to those where lunch, snacks and drinks tastings are included ($140 for 1-8 people). Pick-ups available.
Out and About Wine Tours, T9377 3376, www.outandabouttours.com.au. Relaxed but informative winery tours in the region. Half-day, full-day and twilight tours/cruises.
Swan Valley Shuttle Service, T9274 6569. Offers a good hop-on hop-off service that leaves from the VIC Wed-Sun every hour 0930-1630, $60). Can be booked through the VIC.
Swan Valley Tours and Cruises, T9274 1199, www.svtours.com.au. Offers various wine and gourmet tours and cruises with pick-ups from central Perth or Guildford.
Wagon Winery Trails, T0412 917496, www.swanvalleywa.com. Take the decidedly slow option in horse-drawn pioneer wagons. Lots of different packages, but none go very far from their starting point in Upper Swan. Transfers available from Guildford train station.

⊖ Transport

Swan Valley *p78*
Train There are frequent train services between **Midland**, **Guildford** and **Perth**. Last trains leave Midland Mon-Fri 2400, Sun (ie Sat night) 0130 and Sun 2330.

Perth Hills

The sharp, 400-m-high western escarpment of the Darling Ranges runs parallel to the coast about 30 km inland, forming a natural eastern border to the rapidly expanding Perth suburbs, and a western border to WA's huge and ancient inland plateau. Large areas of the scarp have been set aside as reserves and parks, preserving the characteristic gum woodlands and providing city dwellers and visitors with an extensive network of bush walking, mountain biking and horse-riding tracks. Some of the valleys that snake inland have been cultivated by European settlers to produce fruit, vegetables and grapes. Although not as well known as those in Swan Valley, several wineries have been established, in some of the prettiest settings.

Ins and outs ▸▸ *For listings, see pages 86-88.*

There are some buses from Perth and Midland. An excellent way of getting a flavour of the hills forests is by bike, and there are a number of circular trails. ▸▸ *See Activities and tours and Transport, page 88, for details.*

The main VICs are in **Kalamunda** ⓘ *Library building, Railway Parade, next to History Village, T9293 4872, daily 1000-1600*; and **Mundaring** ⓘ *7225 Great Eastern Highway, T9295 0202, 1000-1600*. **Perth Hills National Park Centre** ⓘ *Allen Rd, off Mundaring Weir Rd, T9295 2244, Mon-Fri 1000-1630*, has brochures and maps for the Bibbulmun Track and Munda Biddi Track, and will advise on current trail accessibility.

Kalamunda → *25 km from Perth, 25 km from Mundaring.*

Kalamunda is a good-sized modern town, seemingly built around a central shopping centre and shoving its history to the fringes. Its main claim to fame is as the northern terminus of the prodigious **Bibbulmun Track**, but the **Kalamunda History Village** ⓘ *Railway Rd, T9293 1371, Mon-Thu 1000-1500, Sat 1000-1200 and Sun 1330-1630, $5, children $2, concessions $4*, is well worth a stroll around. Although a small example of an assembled village, all the dozen or so buildings and their copious contents are authentic and well laid out around the towns original railway station.

Gooseberry Hill and the Zig Zag → *15-km loop driving circuit.*

From Kalamunda it is worth driving out on Williams Street to Gooseberry Hill, where the road winds one-way down to close to the base of the scarp. At almost every point along the series of switchbacks there are sweeping views of the coastal plains and Perth city centre. No entry fees apply. The road comes out on Ridge Hill Road. Turn right, left into Helena Valley Road, right again into Scott Street for the Great Eastern Highway. Turn left, then left again for Kalamunda Road and the Roe Highway.

Bickley Valley

Reached by taking Mundaring Weir Road from Kalamunda and then turning right into Aldersyde Road, Bickley Valley is one of the most picturesque of several small valleys that have been partially cultivated for fruit and wine. Fairly steep-sided, it is a patchwork of native forest, pasture and groves of fruit trees, always with a green, lush feel even in the heat of summer. There are a handful of small wineries dotted along and just off Aldersyde Road and Walnut Road, but they are only open for tastings at weekends. At the far end of the valley is the **Perth Observatory** ① *337 Walnut Rd, T9293 8255, www.perthobservatory.wa.gov.au; day tours 1st Sun in Jun, Jul, Aug and Sep at 1400 (1 hr), other days as per demand, $7, children and concessions $5; viewing nights $20, children and concessions $12, 2 sessions each evening, the last of which sometimes stretches beyond the usual 1 hr*, which regularly holds viewing nights throughout the year. Each month they generally have a week of 'night sky evenings', when the moon is fuller and visible, and a week of 'deep sky nights', when the moon's absence allows even more to be seen, including other galaxies. Parties of 12 usually get to see six objects through three separate telescopes. These evenings are some of the best value of their kind, and bookings are essential. Also available are day tours, more appropriate for children, which include a slide show and sometimes sunspot viewing.

Mundaring → *40 km from Perth, 55 km from Northam.*

Straddling the Great Eastern Highway with its thunderous, constant traffic, Mundaring is a modern town of pale-coloured brick with glimpses of an earlier history peeping through the cracks. Its chief attractions lie outside the town itself, west along the highway at John Forrest National Park, and south at Mundaring Weir. The **VIC** ① *The Old School, 7225 Great Eastern Highway, T9295 0202, www.mundaringtourism.com.au* is able to provide useful information and advice on nearby sights.

John Forrest National Park → *30 km from Perth, 10 km from Mundaring.*

① *$11 per vehicle, T9298 8344. Access is via looping Park Rd, off the highway, a side road taking you into the visitor area where a fee applies. At the visitor area are a few facilities including bush BBQs, picnic tables and a ranger station.*

The first formal reserve in WA, declared in 1900, John Forrest is still one of the biggest parks dedicated to preserving the original wildlife and gum woodlands of the scarp, extending about 4 km along the side of the Great Eastern Highway and 5 km north.

The main draw of the park is its walking trails, best undertaken in winter or spring when the brooks are flowing. It is absolutely riddled with tracks, but many are unmarked so take care to stick to the signposted trails. For a short easy stroll, the **Glenn Brook Trail** takes about 45 minutes from the visitor area and winds its way around the Glen Brook Dam that you will have seen on your right while driving in. The trail is relatively flat, has views across the dam and passes a large number of wildflowers in spring. Considerably more challenging is the **Eagles View Walk Trail**, a six- to seven-hour loop that takes in much of the park's area and scenery. Taking the clockwise option the walk begins with an uphill section to a lookout, with views over the coast plain to Perth, then along a pretty valley that is also thick with wildflowers in spring. The return section undulates over a couple of rocky ridges, once again affording views of Perth, but this time also over much of the park in the foreground.

Mundaring Weir → *8 km from Mundaring, 16 km from Kalamunda.*

In 1895, with the Kalgoorlie goldrushes in full swing, WA's Engineer-in-Chief CY O'Connor, was given the task of supplying water to the new goldfields. Over 500 km inland, in one of Australia's driest areas, the task seemed to many impossible but it simply had to be done to sustain the new cash cow and O'Connor was the man for the job. His solution was simple, but challenged the technology of the day. He proposed building a massive reservoir in the Perth Hills near Mundaring and from there a pipeline all the way to Kalgoorlie. The scheme was widely derided as unworkable, but O'Connor got his green light. The dam, enlarged to 40 m high in the 1950s and still performing its intended purpose, is a testament to his vision and capability, but sadly he didn't live to see it in operation. He killed himself weeks before the initial trials in 1902, a result of the intense pressure and harassment the scheme brought him.

Today a small huddle of buildings sits in the forest to the north of the main dam wall, among them the excellent pub built to cater for the original workers and engineers, and a YHA hostel. Theres also an art and craft gallery that is open on weekends and public holidays. A little beyond the village the **No 1 Pump Station** ① *T9295 2455, Mar-Jan Wed-Sun and public holidays 1000-1600, $5, children and concessions $3, National Trust operated*, utilizes the original pumphouse and carefully details the development of the goldrushes and the building of both dam and pipeline. In the other direction the **Perth Hills National Parks Centre** ① *Allen Rd, T9295 2244, www.dec.wa.gov.au/n2n*, is the place to visit for advice on walking or driving through the Perth Hills. There is also camping here for $9 per person and the Bibbulmun Track passes nearby. The **Kookaburra Cinema** ① *T9295 6190, nightly Nov-Apr, current releases*, has an outdoor screen and seating. In summer, the **Mundaring Weir Hotel** (see Sleeping, page 87) hosts the **Mundaring Weir Summer Festival**, a series of concerts in the hotels outdoor amphitheatre. They are very popular and accommodation rises in price at these times.

There are a few walking trails in and around the weir. The **Weir Walk**, following yellow-collared posts, takes a little less than an hour and winds around the area between the pub and the weir, over the weir (gates close at 1800), around the picnic areas to the south and through the pumping station complex. It formally starts outside the museum but can be started outside the pub. The **O'Connor Trail**, following the green-collared posts, starts opposite the pub at the craft centre, and follows a loop through the forest, past the discovery centre and cinema. Allow about two hours.

Perth Hills listings

For Sleeping and Eating price codes and other relevant information, see pages 10-14.

🛏 Sleeping

Kalamunda *p84*

$$ Kalamunda Hotel, 43 Railway Terr, T9257 1084, www.kalamundahotel.com.au. Built in 1902, has 3 simple upstairs doubles, all en suite with a/c. Downstairs, the traditional bars have been smartly refurbished and the dining room serves a good range of Mediterranean-style meals. Continental breakfast is included in the price. Meals Mon-Sat 1200-1500, 1800-2100, Sun 1000-2100. Cheaper counter meals are available daily 1200-2100 from the bar.

Bickley Valley *p85*

$$$ Brookside Vineyard, 5 Loaring Rd, T9291 8705, www.brooksidevineyard.com.au.

Bibbulmun Track

Started in the 1970s the long-distance Bibbulmun walking trail was last upgraded in 1998 and is now well marked along its entire route. Starting in Kalamunda it winds its way south through North Bannister, Dwellingup, Balingup, Pemberton and Walpole before finally ending up, 963 km later, in Albany. As well as passing through these picturesque towns the track also winds through several reserves and parks, much of the southern forests and some of the spectacular south coast. There are nearly 50 bush campsites en route, each with a simple three-sided timber bunk shelter, picnic tables, water tank and pit toilets. Note that there are no cooking facilities, water needs to be boiled or treated, and there is no toilet paper. None of the shelters are accessible by private vehicle, a great idea on the part of designers. There are also a few B&Bs that offer pick-ups and drop-offs to sections of the track. The whole walk generally takes around six to eight weeks, but few choose to tackle it in a single go. DEC have suggestions for various short-day sections. The track is by far at its best in winter and spring, think twice, and then again before tackling any of it in high summer. There is a two-volume guide to the track and a series of eight maps also dedicated to it, all available at the **Perth Map Centre** (see page 51) amongst other outlets.

For more information see www.bibbulmuntrack.org.au or www.naturebase.net, or contact the **Friends of the Bibbulmun Track** by calling T9481 0551.

Has a charming garden cottage, built and furnished in the style of the adjacent Federation homestead. Open-plan with combined living and bedroom, pot belly stove, en suite bathroom, and veranda. Substantial, full cooked breakfast and evening meals by arrangement. Cheese platter and wine on arrival.

Mundaring p85

$$$$ LooseBox, 6825 Great Eastern Highway, 2 km west of Mundaring, T9295 1787, www.loosebox.com. Everything about this place exudes quality and indulgence. In the garden are 6 luxury chalets, available as part of a lunch or dinner package Wed-Sun, B&B packages are available every day. See Eating for information on the restaurant.

Mundaring Weir p86

$$$-$$ Mundaring Weir Hotel, T9295 1106, www.mundaringweirhotel.com.au. A grand old pub hotel perched on the hill above the weir pump stations, and a favourite Sun destination when a lamb spit-roast is prepared for lunch. The main bars capture a feel for the pubs century of history, but you'll be likely to head for the garden tables. Fresh, inventive meals are mostly cheap, available Mon-Sat 1200-1430, Fri-Sat 1800-2000, Sun 1200-1800. Accommodation is in 9 external motel-style units, each with an open fireplace, grouped alongside the pubs pool. Room/dinner packages only Sun-Thu. Every Sun there a live bush band plays in the beer garden and a spit roast lamb is for sale from 1500 until sold out.

$$-$ Perth Hills Forest Lodge YHA, Mundaring Weir Rd, T9295 1809. A small, relaxed hostel with 36 beds in dorms, twins and singles. General facilities aren't extensive, but clean and comfortable and include a wood-burning stove and well-equipped kitchen. Popular with groups so make sure you ring ahead.

$ Perth Hills National Parks Centre, Allen Rd, T9295 2244. A handful of camping sites, with toilets and hot showers. There's also a camp kitchen. Book before you arrive.

🍴 Eating

Kalamunda *p84*
$$-$ Le Paris-Brest, Haynes St, T9293 2752. Tue-Sun 0700-1730 and public holidays. Something of a cultural oasis in Kalamunda, a small, cheerful Gallic corner providing a patisserie and café, ongoing art exhibitions, and monthly live jazz on their wraparound terrace. Everything is home-made, including all the cakes and ice cream.
$$-$ Thai on the Hill, on the corner of Haynes Rd and Railway Rd, T9293 4312. Tue-Sun 1800-2200. Has a pleasant rich-red formal dining room and serves Thai food with an extensive range of cheaper veggie options. Licensed.

Gooseberry Hill *p84*
$ Le Croissant du Moulin, 169 Railway Rd, T9293 4345. Wed-Sun 0730-1700. Tucked away but what a find. This patisserie, boulangerie and café offers authentic French baking. Breads, pastries, quiches and good coffee. Come for breakfast and tuck in to a croissant or a bowl of hot chocolate.

Bickley Valley *p85*
$$ Packing Shed, 101 Loaring Rd, T9291 8425, almost next door to **Brookside**. Open for lunches and teas, Fri-Sun 1000-1400 and public holidays. The restaurant of the **Lawnbrook Estate**, now much better known for its food than its wine. Essentially a barn with a large brick terrace, the excellent food is country Mediterranean style, spiced with the odd curry.

Mundaring *p85*
$$$ Loose Box, 6825 Great Eastern Highway, 2 km west of Mundaring, T9295 1787, www.loosebox.com. Wed-Sat 1900-2200, Sun 1200-1400. This restaurant, a winner of a constant stream of state and national awards since it opened in 1980, is a century-old weatherboard house, now opened up into several formal dining areas. The seriously expensive cuisine is classical French, with Australian influences, using local produce. Bookings recommended. Recommended.
$ Little Caesars Pizzeria, 7125 Great Eastern Highway, T9295 6611, www.littlecaesars pizzeria.com.au. Wed-Mon 1600-late. World-famous pizzeria with a vast menu, including many seafood and meat options. Vegans, and vegetarians are also well catered for. Visitors have to try one of the dessert pizzas, such as New York pecan pie.

🥾 Activities and tours

Walking
The principal 40-km loop trail heads out from Midland, up the scarp and through John Forrest National Park, steers well clear of the highway and drops around to Mundaring. Much of the return to Midland is along the route of the Old Eastern Railway. From Mundaring a connecting 15-km loop heads south through the state forest to Mundaring Weir.

🚆 Transport

Bus
Metropolitan buses for **Mundaring** leave from the train station at **Midland**. Buses to **Kalamunda** leave Perth City Busport several times a day. There are direct **TransWA** coaches from **East Perth** that call at **Mundaring**, leaving at Mon 0715, Tue, Thu and Sun 0800, Thu 0930, and Fri 0900.

North of Perth

The coastal road north of Perth runs as far as Lancelin at present but work is currently underway to seal the sandy 4WD track between Lancelin and Cervantes. This will create a coastal route all the way from Perth to Geraldton and will bring much change to the string of sleepy fishing and holiday towns between the two cities. Yanchep National Park makes a fine day trip from Perth, with its tranquil lakes and birdlife, but it is worth continuing north for a night in Lancelin. It is windsurfing heaven but people also come for the long expanse of silky dunes that are magical at sunset and only a short walk from the town centre. Inland, the appealing town of Gingin lies on the Brand Highway and can make an interesting stop on the way to or from Geraldton. Further east, the curious settlement of New Norcia straddles the Great Northern Highway. New Norcia is a small community of Benedictine monks living a contemplative life in their grand edifices, as road trains thunder past.

Yanchep National Park → 50 km from Perth, 80 km from Lancelin.

ⓘ $11 per car. Crystal Cave Tours (45 mins) 1030, 1130, 1300, 1400, 1500. Aboriginal Experience (45 mins) Sat hourly 1300-1500, Sun hourly 1400-1600. $10, children $5.

Perched just inland, 15 km away from Perth's northernmost suburbs, lies one of the region's best parks. Encompassing two lakes, **Loch McNess** and the larger **North Lake**, the area was ear-marked as a nature reserve in 1905, but the park has developed slowly since then and has also seen military use. Yanchep has a wide range of attractions for the visitor. Its bush-covered dunes, teeming with Western Grey kangaroos, overlay a large network of limestone caves (see below). There are many walking trails, threading their way through and around heathland, gum woods and wetland, and there are opportunities for overnight hikes, with camping at the far end of North Lake. As well as the wild 'roos there are two animal enclosures, one for kangaroos and emus, and a large koala enclosure where they actually get to live up trees. A few are brought down occasionally during the day to a smaller area where visitors can have their photograph taken with them. The park is also home to dozens of bird species including galahs and black cockatoos.

The park puts on a constant programme of activities, especially in summer; some free, some not (contact the visitor centre for a current programme). Aboriginal performances of dancing, didgeridoo playing and weapon throwing take place regularly throughout the day. There are also cultural talks and demonstrations about the area's traditional Aboriginal lifestyle. Rowing boats on Loch McNess can be hired at the visitor centre. There's public access to two caves. There are regular tours of the **Crystal Cave**, a still active and therefore quite damp cave, or you can book to explore **Yonderup Cave**, now dry.

Occasional adventure caving trips are also organized for Yonderup. Several short walks of around 2 km (one hour) head around Loch McNess and the caves area, all described on the free map. For details of the longer and overnight walks contact the visitor centre. The **VIC** ① *T9561 1004*, is close to the park entrance, next to a kiosk and tearooms.

Lancelin → *Population: 900. 130 km from Perth, 75 km from Gingin.*

At the current end of the coastal highway, the little fishing town of Lancelin has become a firm favourite of windsurfers and kitesurfers (October-May season). The strong dependable off-shore winds are also responsible for the naked dunes that run for a couple of kilometres just inland of the town. They make an excellent venue for sandboarding, and are also used by local trailbikers, four-wheel drivers and tour operators, but they are at their most striking when devoid of traffic and lit up by a strong sunset when they fleetingly turn blush pink. The dunes start about 1 km north of town, and you should arrive about 25 minutes before sunset to get the full effect. The town beaches are not the coast's best but a few decent surf breaks, snorkelling and diving spots help make this a popular destination. The town has all the basic services, including an ATM in the Gull service station. There is no public transport to or from Lancelin. The **VIC** ① *T9655 1100, daily 0900-1800 (shorter hours in winter)*, is located on the main road.

Gingin → *Population: 600. 80 km from Perth, 225 km from Dongara.*

A tiny, picturesque rural town, Gingin sits inside a loop of Gingin Brook and is the centre of a thriving agricultural community. The town has a fine grassy park by the brook and a few lovely old stone buildings, such as **St Lukes Church** (1860) and **Dewars House** (1880), an unusual two-storey private residence. There are a few basic services on Brockman Street, including a post office and general store, and a good pub on Jones Street between the brook and railway line. To the west of Gingin, Gingin Brook Road (32 km) runs between the Brand Highway and the main coast road to Guilderton and Lancelin. Near here is where the **Gravity Discovery Centre** ① *Military Rd, T9575 7577, www.gdc.asn.au, Tue-Sun 0930- 1700, $15, children $10, concessions $12*, can be found. The interactive nature of the exhibits makes this a great option for those with kids. There is the Leaning Tower of Gingin where visitors can climb 222 steps and drop water balloons through special shoots re-enacting Galileos experiment in Pisa, The Cosmology Gallery houses works of art relating to science and evolution, and there is information on black holes, gravity, the Big Bank and so forth. There is a café, as well as an observatory for star gazing.

New Norcia → *Population: 50. 130 km from Perth, 80 km from Gingin.*

New Norcia is one of the most unusual settlements in Australia. A small community of Benedictine monks live a traditional Benedictine life of work and prayer within an astonishingly grand setting on the hot and dry Victoria Plains. The first Bishop of Perth, Dr John Brady, was concerned for the welfare of Western Australia's indigenous people and thought the blessing of civilization and religion would save them. He persuaded two Spanish monks to come to Australia to establish a mission and they set off from Perth on foot for the Victoria Plains in 1846 to do so. Dom Rosendo Salvado, the first Abbot, aimed to encourage local Aboriginal people to become farmers and to educate Aboriginal children within a self-sufficient religious community. Under the second Abbot, Torres, New Norcia became less of a bush mission and more of a monastic community and centre for education. Torres was also an architect and during his short stint from 1901 to 1914 most of the enormous, elaborate buildings were constructed or simple existing buildings, such as the Abbey Church, were given a face-lift. These days there are only seven monks but they employ a workforce of about 60 to keep the place running. Much of the place is off-limits but there is an interesting **museum and art gallery** ① *T9654 8056, www.newnorcia.wa.edu.au, 0900-1630, $10, children under 12 free, concessions $6, daily tours of the town 1100, 1330. $14.50, children under 12 free, concessions $9 (2 hrs), combined tickets are available for $23, children under 12 free, concessions $14-20*, that focuses on the history of the mission and displays some of New Norcia's rare and valuable artwork and treasures. There is also the opportunity to 'Meet a Monk' on weekdays at 1030 and ask questions about monastic life. A shop sells high-quality pottery, souvenirs and items made by the monks, including olive oil and the renowned preservative-free New Norcia bread, baked daily in a wood-fired oven and served in many Perth restaurants. For more information contact the **VIC** ① *T9654 8056, www.newnorcia.wa.edu.au*, at the museum.

North of Perth listings

For Sleeping and Eating price codes and other relevant information, see pages 10-14.

🛏 Sleeping

Yanchep National Park *p89*
$$$-$$ Yanchep Inn, 200 m north of visitor centre, T9561 1001, www.yanchepinn.com.au. Has 14 luxurious motel units, some with spa, and cheaper hotel-style accommodation with communal facilities. Restaurant has extensive wine list.
$$ Yanchep Holiday Village, 56 St Andrews Dr, 10 km from the park near the small coastal settlement of Yanchep, T9561 2244, www.yanchepholidays.com. A small number of self-contained apartments around a central pool area, surrounded by bush. Facilities include BBQs, open fireplaces and laundry.

Lancelin *p90*
$$ Lancelin Beach Hotel, north end of town, T9655 1005, www.lancelinbeachhotel. com.au. Has motel-style en suite rooms and self-contained units. The licensed, mid-range restaurant overlooks the shore. There is also a bar and an outdoor pool with spa.
$$ Lancelin Holiday Accommodation, T9655 1100. Has a few self-contained, 1- to 2-bedroom units. They can also organize

a variety of houses for short stays in the town. No linen provided. Book through VIC.
$$-$ Lancelin Lodge YHA, south end of town, 10 Hopkins St, T9655 2020, www.lancelinlodge.com.au. Has just about everything you look for in a hostel. Great rooms and communal facilities, friendly, pool, volleyball court, lots of freebies including bikes, and excellent local knowledge. They will even pick up from Perth (cost involved). Weekly discounts available. Recommended.

Camping
There are 2 caravan parks, both with on-site vans. The one at the north end, T9655 1115, is also close to the dunes.

Gingin *p90*
$$ Gingin Hotel, 5 Jones St, T9575 2214, www.ginginhotel.com.au. A country hotel with imaginative rustic decor and a lovely outdoor terrace. There are 6 hotel rooms with share facilities and 6 en suite motel units. Pub food and internet available.
$$ The Runners Rest, 182 Cockram Rd, T9575 1414, B&B on a working farm, with self-catering breakfast provided.
$$-$ Liberty Roadhouse, corner of Brand

Highway and Dewar Rd, T9575 2258. Runs the caravan park next door, sites and cabins.

$ Willowbrook Farm, 1679 Gingin Brook Rd, T9575 7566, Powered and unpowered sites for tents and caravans. Complimentary freshly baked scones, home-made jam and cream on Sun morning; just bring a cup of tea or coffee to wash them down.

New Norcia *p90*

$$ Monastery Guesthouse, T9654 8002. 8 comfortable twin en suite rooms around a courtyard within the monastery. The price (a recommended donation) includes 3 meals of the same fare as the monks, although the dining room is separate. Male guests may be asked to eat with the monks. Book in advance, especially at weekends.

$$ New Norcia Hotel, T9654 8034. Built for parents visiting their children in the colleges next door. The exterior is fit for a king but inside it is a pretty simple country pub with 15 tired double and single rooms with shared facilities. Continental breakfast included in price. Facilities include tennis and basketball courts, pool and 9-hole golf course.

Camping

Caravan and Camping, T9854 8097. Self-contained caravan stopover is possible. There are also a 8 powered tent/caravan sites with basic amenities near the roadhouse.

🍴 Eating

Lancelin *p90*

$$$-$$ Lancelin Bay Restaurant, Miragliotta Rd, T9655 2686. Tue-Sun 0900-2100. Serves up breakfast, seafood dishes, coffee and cake. In the evenings the meals become more sophisticated. The outdoor terrace is a mere stones throw from the beach. Licensed and BYO.

$$ Endeavour Tavern, T9655 1052. Daily 1200-1400 and 1800-2000. Characterful,

modern but rustic, with lots of rough timbers and bare antique brick. The pub garden overlooks the shore and ocean. DJs and live music every weekend.

New Norcia *p90*

$$$-$ New Norcia Hotel, see Sleeping. Lunch Mon-Fri1200-1400, Sat-Sun 1230-1430, and dinner Mon-Fri and Sun 1800-2000, Sat 1800-2030. Serves good food, such as grills, seafood and pizzas. At the bar visitors can try the New Norcia Abbey Ale or the Abbey Wine.

There is also a roadhouse where you can get fast food and sandwiches to eat in or take away, open daily 0900-1700.

⛰ Activities and tours

Lancelin *p90*

Desert Storm Adventures, T9655 2550, www.desertstorm.com.au. Runs a jacked-up yellow bus with enormous tyres, claiming to be above and beyond all other 4WDs. Tours into the dunes for a roller-coaster drive and a spot of sandboarding (45 mins $55, children $35; 1 hr, $70, children $50).

Lancelin Surfsports, T9655 1441, www.lancelinsurfsports.com. Sandboard and surfboard hire.

Werners Hot Spot, T0407 426469, www.windsurfwa.com/werner/werner.html. Hire (from $25 per hr) and lessons. Packages including airport transfer available.

🚌 Transport

Bus Some TransWA buses (N1) pass through **Gingin** on their way north, departing **East Perth** Mon-Sat 0830, Fri 1630 and Sun 0930. Other services (N2) head to **Geraldton** via **New Norcia**, leaving Tue, Thu and Sat 0930, Sun 1145. **Integrity**, Wellington St Bus Station, Perth, T1800 226339, T9574 6707, www.integritycoachlines.com.au, also operate a service up the west coast, stopping at **New Norcia** and running on Wed.

Avon Valley

The area just to the east of the Darling Range is threaded through by the Avon River (pronounced as in 'have', not 'grave'), and is a picturesque country of rolling hills, pasture and woodland. Early European settlers soon found it to be one of the most fertile regions around Perth, and substantial urban and agricultural progress was already being made when the gold rushes began in the 1890s. This saw the area's importance increase yet more as a goods marshalling point and the last place to collect water. Some of the oldest towns in WA can be found here, including York, one of the most attractive towns in the state.

Avon Valley National Park ➜ *65 km from Perth, 35 km from Toodyay.*
ⓘ *$11 car, camping $7 per person, both payable at self-registration stations.*
Avon Valley is a pretty and peaceful small park around a section of the Avon River. The steep-sided valley is covered in woodland and granite outcrops. The park has an interesting mix of flora and fauna as it includes the northern limit of jarrah and the wandoo woodland found in drier country to the east. Marri and grass trees are also common in the park. Euros, western grey kangaroos and more than 90 species of bird live in the park. In the 1860s this area was one of the most inaccessible in the Darling Ranges and was used as a hide-out by bushranger Moondyne Joe. More law-abiding types still use it as a hide-out from the city; there are a handful of tranquil camping spots, each with wood BBQs, picnic tables and pit toilets. **Valley Campsite** is the most popular, often used for launching canoes although the river retreats to a series of pools in summer and autumn. The campsites are about 10 km along steep unsealed roads. There are great views over the valley from Bald Hill.

Toodyay ➜ *Population: 800. 85 km from Perth, 27 km from Northam.*
Like York, its more famous southern neighbour, Toodyay (pronounced Two-jay), has retained a fine collection of Victorian buildings, and also sits alongside the Avon. At this point the river is frequently dry, though its setting is one of prettiest in the area, with several low hills surrounding the small town centre. Toodyay is now closely associated with **Moondyne Joe**, the complex bushranger who for some time in his chequered career camped in the hills around the town (see box, page 97).

A visit to the informative **Newcastle Gaol** ⓘ *follow main Stirling Terr west under the railway bridge, turn left and follow to Clinton St, approximately 1 km, Mon-Fri 1000-1500, Sat-Sun 1000-1530, $3*, illustrates Moondyne Joe's story, and gives another grisly reminder about the shocking treatment the early colonial authorities meted out to the local Aboriginals. In the main street is **Connors Mill** ⓘ *Stirling Terr, 0900-1600, $3, entry via the VIC*, a building that had careers both as a flour mill and a mini power station. It has been restored, with authentic machinery, to a semblance of how it probably looked in its flour-grinding days. The **Cola Café** on Stirling Terrace, is well worth a visit to see the extensive collection of Coca-Cola memorabilia on show (see Eating, page 96). The **VIC** ① *T9574 2435, www.toodyay.com, daily 0900-1700*, is adjacent to the mill and also houses a sweet shop.

Northam → *Population: 7000. 95 km from Perth, 500 km from Kalgoorlie-Boulder.*

Chosen early in the 20th century as the main rail junction for the region, Northam is still the Avon Valley's principal service town. Although there is little hard grist for the tourist mill, a stroll around town will reveal many Victorian buildings, several good pubs and the surprisingly wide **Avon River**, bridged for pedestrians by the longest suspension span of its kind in Australia. This pleasant stretch of water also has another claim to fame, the country's only breeding population of introduced white swans, a novel sight to Perth weekenders, more familiar to many international visitors. During the first weekend in August, the town is packed for the **Avon Descent** race, www.avondescent.com.au. The river can get very white in places on its 133-km way downstream, but the start here is noted more for the screams of spectators than participants.

The town has the usual services, mostly along Fitzgerald Street or in the adjacent shopping centre, including a cinema. The **VIC** ① *2 Grey St, T9622 2100, www.visit northamwa.com.au, Mon-Fri 0900-1700, Sat-Sun 0900-1600*, which houses an exhibition on post-war immigration to the area, is by the river and suspension bridge.

York → *Population: 3200. 95 km from Perth, 35 km from Northam.*

In 1830 European settlers from the Swan River Colony explored the country east of the Darling Range and were delighted to find the Avon Valley. It seemed so fertile that Governor Stirling felt that success of his new colony was assured and one of his companions suggested the area be called Yorkshire as the rolling green hills reminded him of home. Land was grabbed eagerly and the district has been a successful agricultural region ever since. Situated by the Avon River, York experienced a short boom in the 1890s when gold was discovered in the east of the state. At the time York was the easternmost rail terminus and the last source of fresh water but was soon passed by when both water and rail reached Kalgoorlie. Northam was chosen as the major rail junction to the goldfields and became the regional centre, leaving York with a magnificent collection of 19th-century buildings to be left in peace for another century. The town is now an appealing, friendly place with museums, cafés, antique shops and bookshops along the main street that draw lots of visitors from Perth at weekends. York is also known for its festivals; vintage cars in July and jazz in October, www.yorkjazz.com.au.

The chief attraction of York is its remarkable 19th-century streetscape, mostly built between 1880 and 1910. It is well worth a stroll up and down the main street, Avon Terrace, and some of the back streets (local guide and architecture expert Adelphe King can be booked for personalized tours, T9641 1799). The most impressive building is the **Town Hall**, an opulent Edwardian hall. Visitors are welcome to explore the building, which is home to the **VIC** ① *81 Avon Terr, T9641 1301, www.yorkwa.org, 0900-1700*. Also prominent are the post office and courthouse, both designed by architect George Temple-Poole in the 1890s and built of brick and Toodyay stone.

The **Old Gaol and Courthouse** ① *132 Avon Terr, T9641 2072, Mar-Jan 1000-1600, $5,* children and concessions $3, are managed by the National Trust. An influx of land-grabbing Europeans naturally dismayed the Aboriginal people of the area who began to attack the new settlers in the mid-1830s. Soldiers were sent to York to protect the settlers so the town had a strong military and later police presence from its earliest days. The complex began as mud-brick in the 1840s and grew into the grand formal buildings of the courthouse in the 1890s. Visitors can stroll through the courthouses, cell block, stables and a troopers cottage dressed in the furnishings of 1867.

Next door is the **York Motor Museum** ① *116 Avon Terr, T9641 1288, 0930-1500, $8.50, children $3.50, concessions $6.50*, a $20 million private collection of classic cars and sports cars whose highlight is its grand prix racers. The cars range from an 1886 Benz to a 1979 Williams FW07 Cosworth. About 50 of them are kept in working order and are driven around the town in age order during the **Festival of the Cars** in July.

In the oldest part of York, the eastern side, is the **Residency Museum** ① *Brook St, T9641 1751, Tue-Thu 1300-1500, Sat-Sun and public holidays 1100-1530, $4, children $1, concessions $3*. The building housing the museum was originally part of York's Convict Hiring Depot and was then the official residency of the towns early magistrates. It now houses a collection of photographs, clothes and household items.

The **Mill Gallery** ① *13 Broome St, T9641 2900, www.theyorkmill.com.au, Mon-Fri 1000-1600, Sat-Sun 1000-1700*, is a large space showcasing paintings, furniture, woodwork and jewellery. There are also some small craft boutiques on the premises and good views from the upper floors of the old mill. There is a shop and a popular café.

Avon Valley listings

For Sleeping and Eating price codes and other relevant information, see pages 10-14.

⬤ Sleeping

Toodyay *p93*
There are a couple of standard hotels in the centre of Toodyay, whilst the majority of B&Bs are some distance away. The VIC has a full list of accommodation.
$$$-$$ Toodyay Caravan Park, Railway Rd, T9574 2612, www.toodyaycaravan parks.com.au. The closest caravan park, it has on-site vans, a strawbale chalet, self-contained cabins, BBQs, a playground and a saltwater swimming pool. There is a path by the river that leads into town.
$$ Pecan Hill B&B, 59 Beaufort St, T9574 2636, www.pecanhill.com.au. A charming B&B with swimming pool and guest lounge with log fire. All rooms are en suite and have access to the veranda. Evening meals can be arranged.

Northam *p94*
$$$ Brackson House, 7 Katrine Rd, T9622 5262, www.bracksonhouse.com.au. A luxurious B&B with spacious, stylish en suite rooms. The guest lounge is furnished with plush sofas, has a library, log fire and internet access. There is also an outdoor spa and a beautiful courtyard.
$$$ Shamrock Hotel, 112 Fitzgerald St, T9622 1092, www.shamrockhotel northam.com.au. Has been splendidly renovated in keeping with its Victorian heritage. The 13 rooms are luxurious without being fussy and types vary from simple en suites to luxury spa with champagne and chocolates included. All have a/c, TV and fridge. Continental breakfast is included. The main bar is uncluttered and comfortable and the food is consistently good. The restaurant is mostly mid-range, open Mon-Sat 1800-2100.
$$-$ Northam Caravan Park, 150 Yilgarn

Av, T9622 1620. On-site cabins and vans, powered tent sites, laundry facilities and BBQ.
$ Northam Guest House, 51 Wellington St, T9622 2301. The most budget-conscious will head here, 30 basic rooms, mostly doubles, twins and singles and use of a kitchen. It ain't pretty but it is clean and secure. Seriously cheap special rates for long-term stays apply.

York *p94*
Unsurprisingly there are a good number of heritage and heritage-style B&Bs in the area, mostly in the **$$$** price range, though bargains can be had off-season (Dec-Mar) when Perth weekenders find it too hot.
$$$$-$$$ The York, 145 Avon Terr, T9641 2188, www.theyork.com.au. An imposing grey structure, with 8 luxury suites in the restored main building and 15 modern en suite terrace rooms. Dinner packages are available, and there's a good restaurant on the ground floor. This is a modern take on period renovation so don't expect to be transported back in time.
$$$ York Cottages, 2 Morris Edwards Dr, T9641 2125, www.yorkwa.com.au/yorkcottages. Modern and fully self-contained more luxurious than their ancient counterparts. Both have open fires, BBQs and can sleep 6-8. There is also an outdoor spa, children's playground and a tennis court.
$$ Settlers House, 125 Avon Terr, T9641 1096, www.settlershouse.com.au. An English bar with comfy red couches in a refurbished 1845 house. The 18 period rooms with en suite and a/c are situated around the courtyard. Continental breakfast included. Good value. The hotel also contains a swimming pool and a restaurant serving mid-range meals every day.
$$-$ Kookaburra Dream, 152 Avon Terr, T9641 2936, www.kookaburradream.com.au. A very pleasant, friendly hostel in a suitably old building with dorms and twins. Good facilities and extras make this the best budget option.

$$-$ York Caravan Park, 2 km north of town on Eighth Rd, T9641 1421. In a peaceful spot, this site has well-equipped on-site vans and helpful management. Theres a camp kitchen and BBQs are available for use.

⊘ Eating

Toodyay *p93*
$$-$ Cola Café, 128 Stirling Terr, T9574 4407, www.colacafe.com.au. Mon-Fri 0900-1630, Sat-Sun 0800-1700. The town's best café, a shrine to that great god of commerce. Styled as an American diner, specialities are burgers and omelettes, shakes, juices and, of course, the great drink itself.

Northam *p94*
$$-$ Mon Petit, 100 Fitzgerald St, T9622 8805. Daily 0700-2200. Offers tapas and light meals. BYO.
$ Café Yasou, 175 Fitzgerald St, T9622 3128, www.cafeyasou.com.au. Mon-Fri 0800-1600, Sat 0800-1200. A stylish organic café that serves tasty Greek and Cypriot dishes.
$ Riversedge Café, in the VIC building. Tue-Thu 0800-1500 and Fri-Sun 0730-1500. The veranda here is a pleasant place for a light lunch or coffee. It hangs over the riverbank.
$ Two Stories Book Café, 80 Fitzgerald St, T9622 2282. Wed-Sun 1000-1700. A second-hand bookshop with tables and sofas dotted around and a counter serving coffee, tea and home-made cakes and snacks.

York *p94*
$$$- $$ The York 145 Avon Terr, T9641 2188, www.theyork.com.au. Wed-Fri 1100-1430 and 1800-2130, Sat 0800-1430 and 1800-2130, Sun 0800-1430. Sophisticated seasonal dishes are served in the dining room overlooking the main street. Early evening tapas and mezze Wed-Sat. Also offers luxury accommodation (**$$$$-$$$**) in recently refurbished rooms.

Moondyne Joe

Englishman Joseph Johns, convicted of stealing food in 1848, was transported to the Swan Valley colony in 1853. A non-violent and slightly eccentric man, his career as a criminal was chequered with many visits to Toodyay and Fremantle prisons (the latter even built him a special 'escape-proof' cell) and as many escapes. As a felon-at-large and bushranger he frequently took to the area near Toodyay, known to the local Aborigines as 'Moondyne' and now the Avon Valley National Park, so gaining his nickname by a sympathetic public. Then, and now, seen as a somewhat comic figure, his final years were actually extremely sad, his mind succumbing to dementia. He was incarcerated in an asylum, but could never be convinced it wasn't prison and still repeatedly escaped until his quiet death in 1900.

$$ Greenhills Inn, 8 Greenhill Rd, 22 km from York along the road to Quairading, T9641 4095. Wed-Thu 1700-2100, Fri-Sun 1200-1400 and 1700-2100. If time and transport allow try to get out to this pub. It's got loads of character, is full of antiques and there are plenty of interesting locals. The restaurant serves excellent Modern Australian meals.

$$-$ Café Bugatti, 104 Avon Terr, T9641 1583. Wed-Mon 0730-1630. A long-established favourite for great coffee and a good range of traditional Italian dishes such as *osso buco* and veal *parmigiana*, and cheap pasta. Warm timber dining room lined with motoring memorabilia.

$ The York Mill Café & Restaurant, The York Mill Gallery, 13 Broome St, T9641 2447. Mon, Tue, Thu 0900-1600, Fri 0900-2100, Sat 0800-2100, Sun 0800-1700. Warm little café within the mill complex making casual food such as burgers and salads.

$ Jules Café, 121 Avon Terr, T9641 1832. Mon-Fri 0800-1630, Sat 0830-1500. A good spot for a bite of lunch with a few tables on the pavement. Wholesome food including falafel, kebabs, veggie sandwiches, home-made pastries, biscuits and muffins. Recommended.

$ Yorky's Coffee Carriage, South St, T9641 1554. Nov-Mar Thu-Sun 1700-2100, Apr-Oct Thu 1000-1530, Fri-Sun 1000-2100. Novel café in a railway carriage parked by the riverbank. Basic outdoor seating and a simple cheap menu of light afternoon meals, burgers, fish and chips, quiche and lasagne.

▲ Activities and tours

Northam *p94*
Northam has become a very popular ballooning destination and there are a couple of companies who arrange flights from Apr-Nov. $270 per person weekdays and $370 per person at weekends, prices include breakfast after the flight.
Avon Valley Ballooning, 100 Fitzgerald St, T9622 8805, www.avb.net.au.
Windward Balloon Adventures, T9621 2000, www.ballooning.com.au.

⊖ Transport

Avon Valley *p93*
TransWA Prospector train service leaves **East Perth** for **Toodyay** and **Northam** (1 hr) 1-2 times a day, continuing on to **Kalgoorlie**. Their GS2 bus service to **Albany** calls at both **Northam** and **York** (2 hrs), departing Mon and Fri at 0900, Tue 1700, Wed 0945, Fri 1800, and Sun 1300.

South of Perth

The coast immediately south of Fremantle is not the state's prettiest and the region sometimes gets dismissed as a serious destination. From Rockingham the scenery improves, however, and both Rockingham and Mandurah do have their charms, not least the dolphins that live in the waters off both cities. There are tours to see or even swim with dolphins, and the experience here or in Bunbury is usually considerably richer than up at Monkey Mia. Inland, the Darling Range continues south and harbours several forested parks and reserves, which reward the time and effort required to visit them.

The coast to Rockingham

There may be a lot of coast between Fremantle and Rockingham, but it's not the sort of coast that need detain you. The area does seem to attract recreational and theme parks, however, and these may be worth a look if time allows.

Araluen Botanic Park ⓘ *362 Croyden Rd off Brookton Highway, T9496 1171, www.araluenbotanicpark.com.au, 0900-1800. $10, children $5, concessions $8*, is thought by many to be the best of its kind around Perth. Set among the waterfalls, rock pools and tall woodland of the hills, the park features exotic species such as magnolias, rhododendrons and camellias and is known for wonderful flower displays. Facilities include BBQs, picnic areas, a restaurant and kiosk. Electric scooters and free wheelchairs available for visitors with impaired mobility and during peak season the *Araluen Train* runs. It's best to visit in spring, especially when the tulips are out.

Aviation Heritage Museum ⓘ *on the corner of Kwinana and Leach Highways, T9311 4470, www.raafawa.org.au, 1000-1600, $10, children $5, concessions $7.50, Bull Creek station is on the Northern Suburbs to Mandurah railway line and from there it's a 10-min walk*, is one of the country's best military aircraft museums, with over 30 planes. There's a selection from the Second World War, including a Lancaster bomber, and several Australian aircraft. A separate wing documents the development of flight and space travel.

Adventure World ⓘ *179 Progress Dr, Bibra Lake, T9417 9666, www.adventure world.net.au, Sep-Apr 0900-1700 (closed Tue-Wed school days), $47, children and concessions $39*, is a theme park incorporating a wildlife park and over 30 fairground rides and attractions. On the same road is **Bungee West** ⓘ *T9417 2500*, offering bungee jumps and abseils down their purpose-built tower.

Rockingham → *Population: 90,000. 30 km from Fremantle and Mandurah.*

The coast south of Fremantle extends along three long bays, each overlooked by suburbs, naval establishments and industry. **Mangles Bay**, the furthest south, is sheltered to the west by **Garden Island** and forms the northern shore of a roughly square peninsula now occupied for the most part by the city of Rockingham and its suburbs. A thin line of dunes or grassy foreshore just separates these developments from the many excellent beaches that slope gently into relatively calm seas. The combination of usually flat water plus afternoon breezes can make southern **Safety Bay** a popular spot for windsurfers. Its foreshore is virtually undeveloped, with just a few beach facilities, including BBQs, toilets and picnic tables around the junction of Safety Bay Road and Malibu Road. **Rockingham Beach**, on the north shore, does have a few cafés and a couple of hotels. The roads leading away from this beach also mark the original commercial centre of the city, though there are larger and more modern shops and services along Read Street in the centre of the peninsula. The waters around the peninsula teem with wildlife and have been declared a marine park, see Penguin Island, below. The **VIC** ① *19 Kent St, T9592 3464, www.rockinghamvisitorcentre.com.au, Mon-Fri 0900-1700, Sat-Sun 0900-1600*, close to Rockingham Beach, acts as an agent for much of the city's holiday homes.

Penguin Island

① *T9591 1333, www.penguinisland.com.au, island ferry $17.50 return, children $14.50, concessions $16.50 (hourly 0900-1500), island cruises $34.50, prices include Discovery Centre entrance. Note the island is closed to visitors from Jun to mid-Sep.*

Just off the southwest corner of the Rockingham Peninsula, opposite the third main beach area off Arcadia Drive, is tiny Penguin Island, known locally as Pengos. Just 1 km long it has the feel of a miniature Rottnest, a similar landscape of scrub overlying undulating dunes on a limestone base. There are no quokkas here, but there are birds by the thousand, including seagulls, shearwaters, terns and a substantial colony of fairy penguins. Because of this riot of birdlife, and also a few visiting sea lions, the island is a sanctuary and is mostly off-limits. You can access many of its beaches, plus the **Island Discovery Centre**, an information kiosk with a small, enclosed amphitheatre behind. At the centre of several rows of seating is a large glass tank, freely accessible to wild penguins, many of which know they'll get a modest feed daily at 1030, 1230 and 1430 (weather permitting). This is well worth a look even though you are likely to see penguins while walking around the island. Another key attraction of the island is the wealth of snorkelling to be done just off its beaches, particularly the eastern ones where there is a small wreck. While on the island you may see sea lions on the beach, and they or dolphins may come and check you out while snorkelling. There are surf breaks on the western side of the island. There are also several cruises around the island to see and swim with the local sea lions.

Serpentine National Park → *55 km from Perth, 30 km from Rockingham.*

This park is named after the river that flows through it and is dammed at two locations. The **Serpentine Falls** are the main attraction and are accessible by an easy 15-minute walk from a picnic site. The falls are not high; the river flows over smooth and gently sloping granite into a pool and is only really impressive after good rains. There is a popular campground on the northeastern side, accessible from the small town of **Jarrahdale**, a timber town for workers cutting jarrah in the area. The park was originally set aside as a flora and fauna reserve in the 1890s when local naturalists realized all their timber would soon be gone. Unfortunately, the reserve only lasted for a couple of decades until the government permitted it to be cleared for orchards but the falls area was preserved. It is a pleasant place for a picnic or walk and just off the main South Western Highway. There are good views of the plain from **Baldwins Bluff**, a walking trail through woodland to the granite bluff above (6 km, two hours).

Mandurah → *Population: 61,000. 110 km from Bunbury, 20 km from Pinjarra.*
Mandurah straddles the Mandurah Estuary, a narrow channel that flows into **Peel Inlet**, an enormous body of water just to the south of the town. Naturally, water activities dominate, and the place is in the process of transforming itself from a sleepy seaside town into an expensive and desirable place to live. During the late 1980s and the 1990s new suburbs were created on the south side of the estuary by digging canals, now full of flashy homes with boats tied at the door. The town has traditionally had a large retiree population and is also popular with WA families during school holidays for boating, fishing and swimming. Mandurah is closely identified with crabs, which can be picked up in the estuary and are celebrated in an annual **crab festival** in March. Dolphins are often seen in the estuary and are the focus for regular boat cruises. Two of the best beaches are **Blue Bay** and **Silver Sands**, both calm swimming beaches.

Mandurah was settled by Thomas Peel in 1830. The name is a corruption of the Noongar word *mandja* meaning meeting 'place'. Peel and others were settlers from the Swan River colony who chose land grants in this area to develop for agriculture. Many surviving buildings such as **Christ's Church** and those of **Café Pronto** date from the 1870-1890s when the town developed, thanks to sawmilling nearby and the arrival of the railway. There are few recognizably old buildings left but the oldest part of town is the land around the junction of Mandurah Terrace, Pinjarra Road and the old bridge. There is a small museum here, **Mandurah Community Museum** ① *3 Pinjarra Rd, Tue-Fri 1000-1600, www.mandurahcommunitymuseum.org, Sat and Sun 1100-1500, by donation,* in school buildings dating from 1900, which has some interesting exhibits and information on local history. The old bridge spans the estuary at the southern end of Mandjar Bay, and the struts underneath are a popular fishing spot. Cross the bridge to see one of Mandurah's oldest buildings, **Halls Cottage** ① *T9535 8970, Sun 1300-1600.* Built in 1832 by farmer Henry Edward Hall, it has been restored and heritage listed. To see more pick up a brochure for the heritage artwalk trail from the VIC. Back on the eastern bank is another old house that once belonged to a local named Tuckey, who had a fish cannery next door. Tuckey's house is now used for a commercial gallery, Emz Art. Another gallery worth a look is the one in the **Mandurah Performing Arts Centre** ① *T9550 3900, www.manpac.com.au, Mon-Fri 0900-1630, Sat 1000-1600, Sun when performance is scheduled, free,* the glass-fronted building that dominates the boardwalk precinct. The **VIC** ① *75 Mandurah Terr, T9550 3999, www.visitmandurah.com, daily 0900-1700,* sits behind the boardwalk at the northern end of Mandjar Bay. Nearby is the **Australian Sailing Museum** ① *22 Ormsby Terr, T9534 7256, www.australiansailingmuseum.com.au, daily 0900-1700, $10, children and concessions $5,* which is really only for the enthusiast. It contains memorabilia and artwork, and has a café.

Down the coast to Bunbury
The 100-odd km south to Bunbury can be covered by heading inland to Pinjarra, with perhaps a diversion to Dwellingup then south on the South Western Highway. Slightly slower is the Old Coast Road. After staying close to the coast for about 10 km, this road cuts slightly inland, the long **Yalgorup National Park** separating it from the sea. The park

preserves a large area of coastal vegetation, particularly tuart and peppermint woodlands, and also encompasses several lakes. The largest of these, **Clifton Lake**, is the very rare home of a colony of **thrombolites** small, dome-like structures built up by the photosynthetic process of billions of microbes. The process involves drawing in water rich in calcium carbonate and this slowly accumulates in layers as the microbes die. (This is a different process to that which forms the stromatolites in Cervantes and Shark Bay, which are basically layers of sediment trapped in slime.) The thrombolites line the wide white shore of Lake Clifton as far as the eye can see and make an arresting site on a fine day. A boardwalk has been built a short way out over the water, ensuring a close-up view of a scene that would have been a lot more common 600 million years ago. To get to the boardwalk follow the sign for the **Cape Bouvard Winery** about 27 km south of Mandurah. The winery, open daily and about 3 km off the highway, is 100 m from the boardwalk and has a large lawn and picnic tables for customers and tasters. A second access point to the park is off Preston Beach Road, about 10 km south of the thrombolites.

Shortly before Bunbury, about 6 km after the turn-off to Binninup Beach, take the right-hand Cathedral Road. The adjacent partly sealed Buffalo Road heads into **Leschenault Peninsula Conservation Park**, another area of preserved coastal vegetation, also with a campground. Cathedral Road is the scenic route into Bunbury, hugging the shore of picturesque Leschenault Inlet and passing early on by a couple of spots where you're likely to see kangaroos. At the end turn right back onto the Old Coast Road then right again after the bridge into Estuary Drive. This brings you out onto Koombana Drive, turn right to head into the centre of Bunbury.

Pinjarra → *Population: 4000. 85 km from Perth, 24 km from Dwellingup.*
A medium-sized service town, Pinjarra straddles both the Murray River and South Western Highway about 20 km inland from Mandurah. There is a long riverside park on the western bank with a few picnic tables and a BBQ next to the pedestrian suspension bridge. Opposite this, and also near the road bridge, is the **Edenvale Complex**. This small group of buildings dates back to the 1880s and includes the impressive house built by a local parliamentarian, Edward McLarty. One of his sons, Duncan Ross, became Premier of WA in 1947 and the house has a long association with state politics. The rear part of the house is a tearoom and much of the rest of the complex is now used for art and craft shops, studios and a small machinery museum. The town's **VIC** ① *Fimmel Lane, T9531 1438, www.pinjarravisitorcentre.com.au, Mon-Fri 0930-1600, Sat-Sun 1000-1500,* is by the railway station where visitors can catch the train to Dwellingup (See page 107 for details of the Hotham Valley Railway). This is also where the **Discover Alcoa Tours** ① *T9530 2400, www.alcoa.com.au, mid-Jan to mid-Dec daily at 0930 and 1st Fri of the month at 1000, bookings essential,* leave from. These free tours take in the bauxite mine, the alumina refinery and the rehabilitation area.

Nearby is **Peel Zoo** ① *Sanctuary Dr, T9531 4322, www.peelzoo.com, Mon-Fri 1000-1600, Sat-Sun 0900-1700,* which is 2 km west of Pinjarra and home to koalas, emus, Tasmanian Devils and kangaroos.

Dwellingup → *Population: 450. 24 km from Pinjarra.*
Still a timber milling town, Dwellingup is a sleepy settlement in the hills surrounded by extensive jarrah forests. Although it has a long history in the timber felling and milling

industry there is little of this heritage left to speak of as most of the town was razed to the ground by a fierce bushfire that swept through in 1961. The focus of the town is now switching more and more to providing activities that best show off the extensive natural attractions around the town, primarily the forest and the Murray River. It is also a stop on the **Munda Biddi Cycle Trail**. Facilities are modest, including a pub, store, post office and an expensive petrol station. See page 107 for details of the Etmilyn Forest Tramway.

North of town the **Forest Heritage Centre** ① *Acacia Rd, T9538 1395, www.forest heritagecentre.com.au, 0900-1600, $5.50, children $2.20, concessions $4.40, 1-hr guided tour $6.60 (minimum 10 people), signposted 1 km from the VIC*, is a leaf-shaped set of buildings showcasing the process of carpentry from forest to furniture. Outside are several bushwalks, from five to 20 minutes long, each focusing on a different aspect of the forest: from canopy viewing, identifying tree species and their Aboriginal use, to wildflowers. Inside are a forest interpretative centre, carpentry workshops and finally a gallery and shop selling exquisite handmade wooden furniture and turned items. West of town the **Marrinup Reserve** is the site of an old Second World War internment camp, now a pleasant picnic and bushwalking spot.

The **VIC** ① *Marrinup St, opposite the pub, T9538 1108, www.murray.wa.gov.au, Mon-Fri 0900-1500, Sat-Sun 1000-1500*, and has a good range of local maps and guides. The local **DEC office** ① *Banksiadale Rd, T9538 1078, 0800-1630*, is close by.

Lane Poole Reserve
① *T9538 1078, camping $7, children $2, concessions $5, maximum 14 days' camping during school holidays, detailed map and guide available at the VIC, the best time to visit the forests around Dwellingup is spring and autumn.*
South of Dwellingup, 7 km down Nanga Road, is the northern boundary of Lane Poole Reserve, an extensive area of pretty jarrah and marri forest through which the Murray River runs for several dozen kilometres. There are a number of bush and riverside campsites, most with fireplaces, picnic tables and toilets. The Bibbulmun Track (see box, page 87) passes through the reserve and the river, though long and flat in parts, has some stretches of white water. There are also other walking and mountain-biking trails, and lots of swimming spots. The roads within the reserve are unsealed.

Dryandra Woodlands → *160 km from Perth, 140 km from Dwellingup.*
Dryandra is within the wheatbelt region and is a vital remnant of the kind of vegetation that used to cover the area before it was cleared for farming. The reserve is formed from 17 blocks of bush and is a major focus of conservation in the state. Species of mammals that were nearly extinct have been saved by Western Shield, a DEC programme of wildlife conservation, involving fox control and breeding enclosures. The park is best known for the numbat, an ant- and termite-eating marsupial that feeds in daylight hours but is difficult to see because of its keen senses of hearing and smell. This striped creature looks a bit like a large squirrel and can stand on its hind legs. You'll need to stay upwind or it will scamper off as soon as it gets a whiff of you. Other rare animals of the Dryandra are the woylie and tammar wallaby. The reserve is also a haven for birds and birdspotters have counted about 130 species here. The woodland is open, consisting mostly of wandoo, powderbark and brown mallet, with many walking trails. It is a special place where you may see some of WA's rarest animals if you are patient. Probably your best chance of

Fairy penguins

Also known as Little Penguins, these tiny birds, the world's smallest penguins, have colonies right around Australia's southern coasts. The Penguin Island colony is the largest in WA with about 600 breeding pairs. They like to nest in small natural caverns, under thick vegetation or in sand burrows.

They spend most of the day out at sea feeding, normally only coming in at dusk or even remaining out at sea for several days. Activity on land increases around March when they start to get frisky. Egg laying happens from May to October with incubation taking about 35 days.

seeing some of Dryandra's shy nocturnal creatures, such as the bilby, western barred bandicoot, hare-wallaby and burrowing bettong, is to join a guided night tour from the **Barna Mia Centre** ① *T9881 9200 or T9881 2064, tours begin after sunset on Mon, Wed, Fri and Sat, $13, children $7, families $35, book before 1600.* The nearest town to pick up supplies is Narrogin, a large farming community 27 km east, and you can get DEC brochures on Dryandra from the Narrogin VIC ① *corner of Fairway and Park Sts, T9881 2064, Mon-Fri 0900-1700, Sat 1000-1600, Sun 1100-1500.*

South of Perth listings

For Sleeping and Eating price codes and other relevant information, see pages 10-14.

● Sleeping

Rockingham *p98*
Self-contained apartments, units and holiday homes are the big thing in Rockingham. Many apartments and homes can only be rented by the week, contact the VIC for options. There are a number of B&Bs in town, all priced around **$$$-$$**.
$$$$-$$$ Beachside Apartment Hotel, 58 Kent St, T9529 3777, www.beachsideapartment. com.au. At the top end of the market with several smart modern 1- to 3-bedroom apartments overlooking the Rockingham foreshore and beach. The enclosed **Y2K Café Restaurant** offers various meals, BYO possible.
$$$ Manuel Towers, 32A Arcadia Dr, Shoalwater, T9592 2698, www.manueltowers. com.au. A little way out of town with views over the ocean, the Penguin room overlooks Penguin Island. Forget Fawlty Towers and

think courtyard garden, relaxing atmosphere and a killer breakfast.
$$ CWA Apartments, 108 Parkin St, T9527 9560, 200 m back from northern Palm Beach. At the budget end of the market.

Mandurah *p100*
Most accommodation in town is holiday units and houses. Contact the VIC for more options as it acts as a booking service. Thanks to Mandurah's proximity to Perth, occupancy and prices rise at weekends and on public and school holidays. Book ahead at these times.
$$$$-$$$ Dolphin Houseboats, Ocean Marina, T9535 9898, www.dolphinhouseboats.com. Attractive and comfortable 4-, 6-, 8- or 10-berth houseboats. Most with bunks, kitchen, bathroom and eating area. Price applies to boat so good value for 4-8 people. Prices rise steeply for weekends and public holidays.
$$$$-$$$ Quest Apartments, 20 Apollo Pl, T9535 9599, www.questmandurah.com.au.

Elegant serviced apartment complex on the southern shore. Apartments have 1-3 bedrooms and full kitchen, complex also has BBQs, pool, spa and boat pens.

$$$$-$$ Atrium, 65 Ormsby Terr, T9535 6633, www.atriumhotel.com.au. Multi-storey hotel with 117 smart a/c rooms around a central atrium furnished with plants and an indoor pool. There are also self-catering apartments here and a restaurant, outdoor pool, BBQs, tennis courts, saunas. 24-hr reception.

$$$-$ Mandurah Caravan & Tourist Park, 522 Pinjarra Rd, T9535 1171, www.mandurah caravanpark.com.au. A large park with chalets and cabins, pools, kiosk, BBQ areas, Wi-Fi and playground. There's even a crab cooker.

$$ Belvedere Caravan Park, 153 Mandurah Terr, T9535 1213. Small, quiet caravan park close to town centre with on-site vans and cabins. BBQ areas available, dogs are allowed by prior arrangement only.

$$ Foreshore Motel, 2 Gibson St, T9535 5577, www.mandurahwa.com.au/foreshoremotel. Good location a few steps from the foreshore café strip, a/c rooms with TV, phone, fridge, tea/coffee.

Pinjarra p101

$$$$ Lazy River B&B, 9 Wilson Rd, T9531 4550, www.lazyriver.com.au. Enjoy the peace and quiet, kayak on the river, fish or just read the paper. The 4 rooms are well-appointed and some have 4-posted beds. Complimentary champagne and canapés are provided in the evening, and a breakfast hamper is included in the price. A 3-course evening meal is available on request for $60 per person, handy if you don't want to drive anywhere.

$$$-$$ Pinjarra Motel, South Western Highway, T9531 1811, www.pinjarramotel.com.au. Standard and deluxe motel rooms, a swimming pool and a fully licensed restaurant.

$$-$ Fairbridge Village, 10 km up the highway, T9531 1177, www.fairbridge.asn.au.

A large activity and education centre, the renovated timber cottages once housed English orphans. Now catering mainly for large groups, they have a few self-contained cottages (sleeping 2-56) that are good for families and small groups. Facilities include a snack shop, free sports (swimming, tennis, and adventure playground), bushwalks and BBQs. No linen provided.

$$-$ Pinjarra Cabins and Caravan Park, 1716 Pinjarra Rd, T9531 1374, www.pinjarracaravanpark.com.au. A short distance out of town. Tent sites, cottages and cabins. There's also a pool and a nearby golf course.

Dwellingup p101

There are a handful of B&Bs in the forest surrounding the town.

$$$ Milltree Cottage, T9447 5686, www.dwellingupaccommodation.com.au. A self-contained cottage with 3 bedrooms surrounded by jarrah trees, sleeping up to 8. Facilities include BBQ, TV and a/c. Minimum stay of 2 nights.

$$-$ Dwellingup Community Hotel/Motel, Marrinup St, T9538 1056. A large, friendly open-plan pub with cheap counter meals, bands during the Sun afternoon sesh, cheap hotel rooms, including singles, and a few external motel rooms. Meals daily 1200-1400, Mon-Sat 1800-2000.

Lane Poole Reserve p102

$$-$ Nanga Bush Camp, T1800 801807, www.nangabush.com. Just by the entrance to the reserve (follow the main road around to the right across one-lane bridge), and right by the river. Primarily catering for large school groups, they have a few self-contained bush cabins, expensive for 1-2 people, good value for 6-10.

Dryandra Woodlands p102

There are good campsites at Congelin Dam.

$ Dryandra Woodland Village, T9884

5231, www.dryandravillage.org.au. Comfortable self-contained accommodation within the reserve in the settlement. Simple but charming timber workers cottages are equipped with a full kitchen and BBQ but own linen required. The smaller cottages sleep 2, 4, 10 and 12 and there is a complex that caters for large groups up to 56.

🍴 Eating

Rockingham *p98*

With so much ocean it's a shame not to eat within sight of it.

$$$ Emmas on the Boardwalk, The Boardwalk, 1 Railway Terr, T9592 8881, www.emmasontheboardwalk.com.au. Wed-Sun 1200-1400 and 1800-2100. A Modern Australian restaurant serving quality food. The service is impeccable and the views over the ocean an added bonus.

$$-$ Bettyblue Bistro, The Boardwalk, just along from **Emmas**, T9528 4228. Tue-Sun 0900-late. Good views over the water and a popular choice for breakfast, lunch or dinner, specializes in seafood. Weekdays there is a $25 dinner special in low season.

$$-$ Winstons, T9527 1163, on the main Rockingham Rd cappuccino strip. Daily 0800-2030. Snacks and coffee outside of main mealtimes. Pavement tables.

$ La Gelateria, corner Rockingham Beach Rd and Railway Terr. A mid-range café with an excellent range of ice cream. It also serves good coffee and a variety of sweet treats.

$ Pengos, 153 Arcadia Dr, Shoalwater Bay, at the ferry terminal opposite Penguin Island, T9592 6100. Sun-Thu 0700-1700, Fri-Sat 0700-1900. A simple café serving seafood and burgers. Also offers a range of salad options, and is good stop for breakfast or a coffee and cake.

Mandurah *p100*

Picnic tables and free BBQs on the foreshore.

$$ Café Pronto, on the corner of Mandurah Terr and Pinjarra Rd, T9535 1004, www.cafepronto.com.au. Daily 0700-2100. One of the best places to eat in town, this relaxed brasserie takes up 2 historic old houses on a busy corner. Food is a good mix of seafood, steak and Asian dishes like curries, stir-fries and warm salads. Also more snacky light meals (cheap), wood-fired pizzas and extensive all-day breakfast menu.

$$ M on the Point, 1 Marco Polo Dr, T9534 9899, www.m-onthepoint.com.au. Daily 0700-late. A popular restaurant and bar with a spacious terrace overlooking the water. There is a choice of casual food, such as hot pork rolls or pizza, or more filling pasta dishes, burgers or seafood. Cocktails, early evening specials and live music at weekends. More of pub atmosphere than a restaurant. Half-price Wed (casual menu only) attracts a lot of people.

$ Cicerellos, 73 Mandurah Terr, T9535 9777, www.cicerellos.com.au. Daily 1030-2030. A branch of the famous Fremantle restaurant, this place offers upmarket fish and chips and is licensed but has no table service. Pleasant balcony tables upstairs, overlooking the bay. Also takeaway.

$ Foreshore Takeaway, 25 Mandurah Terr. Fish and chips to eat on the grass opposite.

$ Penang House, 45 Mandurah Terr, T9535 8891. Daily 1645-2000. One of the towns most popular restaurants. Good Chinese and Malaysian dishes under $20. BYO.

$ Ruffinos, Scotts Plaza, 52 Mandurah Terr, T9534 9906, www.mymandurah.com/ruffinos. Tue-Thu 1700-late, Fri-Sun 1100-late. Italian family restaurant with 18 types of pizza and 30 varieties of pasta. Italian mains are mid-range. Leave room for the gelato. Fully licensed, BYO wine only.

$ Taku Japanese Kitchen, Scotts Plaza, 52 Mandurah Terr, T9582 7308. Tue-Sun 1130-1430, Tue-Sat 1700-2100, Sun 1700-2030. Small dining room and cheap sushi, sashimi, noodles and teriyaki meats. Also takeaway.

Cafés

The Merchant Tea & Coffee Co, 9
Mandurah Terr, T9535 2634. Daily 0730-2100.
A franchise café but one of Mandurah's most
popular, with a terrace overlooking the water.
Good coffee and cakes, and light meals
(cheap).

Simmo's Icecream, Boardwalk, T9582 7177,
www.simmos.com.au. Mon-Fri 1000-1700,
Sat 1000-1800, Sun 1000-1730. Ice creams,
plus waffles, coffee and drinks in an attractive
room overlooking the bay.

Pinjarra *p101*
$ Edenvale Tea Rooms, in the Edenvale
complex, T9531 2223. Open daily around
1000-1600 for lunch and afternoon teas.

Dwellingup *p101*
$$ Millhouse, McLarty St, T9538 1122.
Mon-Thu and Sun 0830-1600, Fri-Sat
0830-2000. The towns little touch of class,
a chic restaurant, café and chocolate-maker.

▲ Activities and tours

Rockingham *p98*
Diving and snorkelling
Pick up a copy of the *Diving & snorkelling*
guide from the VIC, as it details all the nearby
sites. The diving shops in town offer PADI
courses and boat dives. Alternatively, there
is the self-guided **Rockingham Wreck Trail**
(you need a buddy to dive this).
Subanautics Diving, 33 Dixon Rd, T9524
4447, www.scubanautics.com.au. Boat dives
out to the marine park. Also runs courses
and hires out equipment.

Dolphin cruises
The bays around Rockingham are home to
about 130 dolphins, many of whom have
been become friendly to people.
Rockingham Wild Encounters, T9591 1333,
www.rockinghamwildencounters.com.au.
Runs 2 excellent tours to see them, both
operating daily between mid-Sep and May.

Dolphin Watch Eco-Adventure ($65, children
$50-60) leaves the Yacht Club jetty, the
Esplanade, Rockingham, at 0830, returning
about 1100. Swim with Dolphins Tour ($205
including snorkelling gear, wetsuits and lunch)
leaves the jetty at 0730, returning around
1100-1500. There are Perth bus pick-ups for
both tours from the Wellington St Bus Station
(costs a bit more). Booking essential. Wild
Encounters also offers tours to
Penguin and Seal Island.

Kayak tours
Capricorn Kayak Tours, T6267 8059,
www.capricornseakayaking.com.au. Takes
small groups out sea kayaking around some
of Penguin and Seal islands best offshore
spots, past colonies of sea lions, pelicans and
Fairy Penguins. Also includes a guided walk of
Penguin Island. Equipment, morning tea and
lunch. Pick-ups are available from Perth and
Fremantle, or meet near Pengos. Full-day
tours from Nov-Mar, $149.

Mandurah *p100*
Boat hire/cruises
A free *Mandurah Boating Guide* is available
at the VIC, with a map of local waters and
details of boating regulations.
Blue Manna Boat Hire, Mandurah Ocean
Marina, T9535 5399, www.bluemanna
boathire.com.au. Has 8-seater runabouts
for hire ($45 for 1 hr). Standard pontoons
are $65 for 1 hr, deluxe $85.
Mandurah Boat Hire, Mandurah Terr,
T9535 5877. Sep-May 0800-sunset, Jun-Aug
0900-sunset. Has runabouts and punts for
hire, plus bicycles. Pontoons $50 per hr,
dinghies $80 per hr (4 people), bicycles
$10 per hr.
Mandurah Ferry Cruises, 73 Mandurah
Terr, opposite the VIC, T9535 3324,
www.mandurahferrycruises.com.
Sep-May Tue-Sun 1030-1530. Good-value
half-day cruise up the Murray River, past
canals, dolphins and the Peel Inlet, 3-course

lunch at a restaurant en route included and a trip aboard the historic the *Peel Princess*. $72, children $47, concessions $66. Tickets on board or at office opposite the VIC.

Diving
Noted for wreck dives. Ask at the VIC or dive shops for locations and advice.
David Budd Diving Academy, The Plaza Shopping Centre, corner of Mandurah Terr and Tuckey St, T9535 1520, www.davidbudd diving.com.au. Offers hire, lessons and great friendly advice. A Rottnest double dive with full gear and lunch is $198.

Family
On the other side of the river there is a summer theme park with crazy golf, ferris wheel, and all the usual entertainment. A special runs on Fri night with a happy hour from 1900-2200 where a $16 ticket will give unlimited ride access.
Just4Fun Aqua Park, Western Foreshore, T0422 439008, www.just4funaquarpark.com. Open Nov-April. Water activities and paddle boats for the whole family, day passes $40.

Fishing/crabbing
Blue Manna crabs can be caught in the Peel Inlet and Mandurah Estuary in summer and autumn. The Fisheries Department of WA sets rules on methods, size and quantity, check with the VIC. Equipment can be hired from the boat-hire businesses.
Aqualib Marine Charters, T9586 9778, www.aqualib.com.au. Game fishing, deep-sea fishing and 3-day Rottnest Excursion available. Prices include lunch, tackle and bait. Call ahead to check if trips are running as minimum numbers are needed.

Golf
There are 2 major golfing resorts, both north of Mandurah.
Meadow Springs Golf & Country Club, Meadow Springs Dr, T9581 6002,

www.msgcc.com.au. Bushland golf course.
Secret Harbour Golf Links, Secret Harbour Blvd, T9524 7133, www.secretharbourgolf links.com.au. Links course.

Pinjarra *p101*
Hotham Valley Railway, T9221 4444 (Perth office), www.hothamvalleyrailway.com.au. From the railway station over the river the *Steam Ranger* heads up to Dwellingup Wed and Sun at 1030. After a 2-hr stopover visitors hop back on and return to Pinjarra for 1600 ($40, children $20). The *Dwellingup Forest Train* departs Dwellingup station Sat-Sun and public holidays at 1100 and 1400 (weekdays by prior arrangement) to Etmilyn Siding ($18, children $9). Theres also an evening train on Sat at 1945, this journey includes a 5-course meal in the vintage dining car ($75). Bookings in advance recommended for all journeys and essential for the evening ride.

Dwellingup *p101*
Dwellingup Adventures, corner Marrinup and Newton Sts, T9538 1127, www.dwellingupadventures.com.au. Organizes a variety of self-guided rafting and canoeing tours along the Murray. They range from half-day excursions (from $97 for a 2-person canoe), to overnight canoe adventures (from $192 for a 2-people canoe). Guided rafting trips along the Murray River depart every Sun ($130 per person, including hot soup), Hires camping gear, mountain bikes and kayaks.
School of Wood, based in the Forest Heritage Centre, T9538 1395, www.forestheritagecentre.com.au. The school runs introductory courses (160 hrs for $215) alongside their 2-year diplomas. Participants come away with their own self-made box, chair or even mandolin, constructed from the finest WA or Tasmanian timbers, and for around half the cost you'd see it in a shop. It also offers a variety of other creative workshops, prices start from about

$165 per course. Contact the centre for a programme.

⊖ Transport

Rockingham *p98*
Bus Rockingham lies under the umbrella of Perth's metropolitan bus network. There are frequent services daily: north to **Perth**, south to **Mandurah**, and also various routes around the peninsula. The main bus station is in the centre of the peninsula on the corner of Council Av and Clifton St. Aside from the metropolitan services, Rockingham lies on both **TransWAs** and **South West Coachlines** (T9324 2333, www.southwest coachlines.com.au) main southbound routes. Some **TransWA** services, which leave from the central Read St shopping centre, head for **Bunbury**, **Busselton**, and the Cape-to-Cape towns. Other buses call at Bunbury before heading through the Timber Towns to **Pemberton**. South West Coachlines have similar though shorter services, daily to **Dunsborough**, Mon-Fri to **Manjimup**.

Penguin Island *p99*
Ferry A ferry leaves for the island from the Mersey Point Jetty, Shoalwater Bay, every hour, daily 0900-1500, last return 1600. Return tickets cost $12 or $17.50 and include Discovery Centre entry, children $16.50. The ferry does not operate Jun-Sep as the island is closed to visitors.

Serpentine National Park *p99*
Train TransWA's *Australind* train line stops at **Serpentine** on its way to **Bunbury**. Services leave Perth daily.

Mandurah *p100*
Bus TransWA bus services leave from the corner of Sutton and Davey Sts for **Bunbury**, **Busselton**, and the Cape-to-Cape towns, while others call at Bunbury before heading through the Timber Towns to **Pemberton**. South West Coachlines have similar, shorter services, **Dunsborough** and **Manjimup**. There are services from Dower St to **Rockingham** (connections to **Fremantle** Mon-Fri only) and **Perth**.

Train Trains on the Mandurah line leave regularly every day to/from the underground terminal of **Perth** train station (50 mins).

Pinjarra *p101*
Train TransWAs *Australind* train line stops at **Pinjarra** on its way to **Bunbury**. Services leave Perth daily.

❶ Directory

Mandurah *p100*
Banks Major banks have branches and ATMs on Pinjarra Rd. **Internet** Lasar, 264 Pinjarra Rd, T9535 3947, Mon-Fri 0900-1730, Sat 0900-1300, internet access, printing and scanning. **Medical services** Peel Health Campus, 110 Lakes Rd, T9531 8000. **Police** 333 Pinjarra Rd, T9581 0222. **Post** 30 Pinjarra Rd.

Contents

Footnotes

Index

Titles available in the Footprint *Focus* range

Latin America	UK RRP	US RRP
Bahia & Salvador	£7.99	$11.95
Buenos Aires & Pampas	£7.99	$11.95
Costa Rica	£8.99	$12.95
Cuzco, La Paz & Lake Titicaca	£8.99	$12.95
El Salvador	£5.99	$8.95
Guadalajara & Pacific Coast	£6.99	$9.95
Guatemala	£8.99	$12.95
Guyana, Guyane & Suriname	£5.99	$8.95
Havana	£6.99	$9.95
Honduras	£7.99	$11.95
Nicaragua	£7.99	$11.95
Paraguay	£5.99	$8.95
Quito & Galápagos Islands	£7.99	$11.95
Recife & Northeast Brazil	£7.99	$11.95
Rio de Janeiro	£8.99	$12.95
São Paulo	£5.99	$8.95
Uruguay	£6.99	$9.95
Venezuela	£8.99	$12.95
Yucatán Peninsula	£6.99	$9.95

Asia	UK RRP	US RRP
Angkor Wat	£5.99	$8.95
Bali & Lombok	£8.99	$12.95
Chennai & Tamil Nadu	£8.99	$12.95
Chiang Mai & Northern Thailand	£7.99	$11.95
Goa	£6.99	$9.95
Hanoi & Northern Vietnam	£8.99	$12.95
Ho Chi Minh City & Mekong Delta	£7.99	$11.95
Java	£7.99	$11.95
Kerala	£7.99	$11.95
Kolkata & West Bengal	£5.99	$8.95
Mumbai & Gujarat	£8.99	$12.95

Africa & Middle East	UK RRP	US RRP
Beirut	£6.99	$9.95
Damascus	£5.99	$8.95
Durban & KwaZulu Natal	£8.99	$12.95
Fès & Northern Morocco	£8.99	$12.95
Jerusalem	£8.99	$12.95
Johannesburg & Kruger National Park	£7.99	$11.95
Kenya's beaches	£8.99	$12.95
Kilimanjaro & Northern Tanzania	£8.99	$12.95
Zanzibar & Pemba	£7.99	$11.95

Europe	UK RRP	US RRP
Bilbao & Basque Region	£6.99	$9.95
Granada & Sierra Nevada	£6.99	$9.95
Málaga	£5.99	$8.95
Orkney & Shetland Islands	£5.99	$8.95
Skye & Outer Hebrides	£6.99	$9.95

North America	UK RRP	US RRP
Vancouver & Rockies	£8.99	$12.95

Australasia	UK RRP	US RRP
Brisbane & Queensland	£8.99	$12.95
Perth	£7.99	$11.95

For the latest books, e-books and smart phone app releases, and a wealth of travel information, visit us at: www.footprinttravelguides.com.

footprinttravelguides.com

Join us on facebook for the latest travel news, product releases, offers and amazing competitions: www.facebook com/footprintbooks.com.